May I Hebb Your Attention Pliss

Arnab Ray also known as Greatbong (http://greatbong.net) is one of India's most widely read bloggers, having won the publicly voted Indibloggies 'Blog of the Year' in 2006 and 2008. He has written for the *Washington Post*, *Outlook* and *Indiatimes*. He graduated from Jadavpur University as a Bachelor in Computer Science and Engineering and went on to finish his PhD in Computer Science from State University of New York at Stony Brook. He is presently employed as a research scientist and resides in the suburbs of Washington DC.

May I Hebb Your Attention Pliss

ARNAB RAY

HarperCollins *Publishers* India
a joint venture with

New Delhi

First published in India in 2010 by
HarperCollins *Publishers* India
a joint venture with
The India Today Group

ISBN: 978-81-7223-937-4

2 4 6 8 10 9 7 5 3

HarperCollins *Publishers*
A-53, Sector 57, Noida 201301, India
77-85 Fulham Palace Road, London W6 8JB, United Kingdom
Hazelton Lanes, 55 Avenue Road, Suite 2900, Toronto, Ontario M5R 3L2
and 1995 Markham Road, Scarborough, Ontario M1B 5M8, Canada
25 Ryde Road, Pymble, Sydney, NSW 2073, Australia
31 View Road, Glenfield, Auckland 10, New Zealand
10 East 53rd Street, New York NY 10022, USA

Typeset in 11/14 Weiss
InoSoft Systems

Printed and bound at
Thomson Press (India) Ltd.

MAY I HEBB YOUR ATTENTION PLISS WILL CHANGE YOUR LIFE

Do you have malignant head lice?

Did you lose everything in the global financial meltdown?

Are you having problems with alcohol?

Did you fudge your company's balance sheet and then get caught?

Regret that unprotected night of passion at the truck stop with toothless Chandramukhi?

Did the Taliban just take over your town?

Does your son spit in your face?

Does your daughter call you a jerk?

And more importantly, do you agree with her?

Do not worry. *May I Hebb Your Attention Pliss* is here.

In ten days, it will change your life. Guaranteed. And if by any chance you are not satisfied with this book, you can get your life back.

No questions asked.

Need further motivation? Well then listen to what satisfied readers are saying.

TESTIMONIAL 1

Promila: My husband was coming home every night from work with lipstick on his shirt and the strong lingering scent of woman's perfume. One day I even found lingerie in his briefcase. I cried and cried thinking there is someone else in his life. Then Hemnalini Aunty told me to buy *May I Hebb Your Attention Pliss*.

In just ten days, everything changed. I found out the truth.

The lingerie, the lipstick and the woman's perfume were not of any woman.

They were all my husband's! It's just that he likes to dress like a woman from time to time. What a relief! My marriage has now been saved. Thanks to *May I Hebb Your Attention Pliss*.

TESTIMONIAL 2

Mother: Our son was rotting in jail on a small matter of smuggling in plastic explosives with the ISI mark. Not only was he not getting humane treatment inside jail, but we had been told that he had become the prison-wife of a man named danda-bhai. We used to cry ourselves to bed. Who will marry our son ever?

Father: Then we bought *May I Hebb Your Attention Pliss*. Now our son is safe with us. You see, we smuggled in a small saw between the pages of the book and he used it to file through the windows and escape. Thanks to the book, our son can walk again. Really. He can walk again.

TESTIMONIAL 3

Samuel: We were having problems having a child. Our marriage was breaking up. Then we ran into an old friend of my wife, Rajesh. He gifted me *May I Hebb Your Attention Pliss* and told me to read it alone at night while he took my wife out on his bike to various resorts. Nine months later, we are having our first baby, our marriage is as solid as ever and Rajesh is a close family friend. All of this because of one book. One book that will change your life. Forever.

So what are you waiting for?

Pick up that wallet and buy this book.

I won't regret it.

The 'Nut' Shell

'I will kill him if that's the last thing I do,' he whispered as he picked himself off the warm asphalt, blood dripping down his split temple as the oppressive Kanpur sun beat down mercilessly on him.

Don't you just hate books that start off like this? They drop you in the middle of the action without a compass, leaving you, the reader, the onerous task of having to wade through pages and pages of text before you have any idea about who he is, why he is bleeding, whom he intends to kill, or for that matter, what he is doing in Kanpur.

I do. And that is why I am going to tell you, straight up, what this book is all about.

It is about what I think on a variety of topics – politics, movies, moral policing, call centres, pyramid schemes, toilet flushes...

'Wait ... wait,' you say. 'Why should I care about what you think? After all opinions are like posterior body orifices. Everyone has got one. What is it that is *so special* about you that I should spend good money to buy this book?'

The answer is simple.

Nothing.

I am a most ordinary, politically neutral (and possibly also neutered), pop-culture-crazed Indian guy, who grew up in the '80s and the '90s. That is precisely why I expect that my opinions and my sense of humour will find resonance with many, hopefully leading them to chuckle and perhaps even guffaw, at least once or twice, during the course of this book and exclaim out loud:

'Yep that is exactly how I feel.'

Did the explanation above make things absolutely clear?

Perhaps not.

So let me try to make my point in another way – by defining what this book is not.

This is not, by any stretch of the term, scholarly work. In other words, very little research was done to produce it. Its pages are in general bereft of numbers, statistics and the other inscrutable artifices of pedantry. And most importantly, no attempt has been made to analyse anything of any importance.

In that respect, this book is very much like your favourite cable news channel. Which is why I hope you shall like it.

The reason why this book lacks any academic rigour is because I am simply not up to it. Brainwise. Blame my stunted intellectual growth, if you will, on my listening to Bappi-da's famous song 'You are my chicken fry, you are my fish fry' (movie name *Rock Dancer*, for those of you who like useless trivia) in an infinite loop for many years. Or blame it on my school's insistence that I memorize the length of the all the major rivers of Africa to the second decimal place for my Class 7 Geography examination.

However, things being as they are, I have to leave the task of writing serious books about flat worlds, argumentative elephants with cellphones and fakirs with laptops to greater minds. More specifically to those who have a Nobel Prize, a Padma Shri or at least have held a position at the United Nations.

Which explains why no attempt is made to compare India with China or to analyse the socioeconomic factors that make us a more corrupt country than Sweden. Neither do I try to answer why desis talk so much nor ponder whether Jinnah was secular.

Instead I talk about the great Bulla rakshas, management institutes, scene punching, Khanna Lahiri Patel Desperation (also called KLPD), Desibaba, serial slapping and various other things you always wanted to know but did not know you wanted to ask.

So have I shed some light on what this book is about?

Possibly not to the extent you thought I would have. But then again, if I tell you the whole story in the trailer itself, why would you even try to download the movie illegally off the Net?

As you may have guessed, the reason for this preamble was simply to grab your attention, hopefully intriguing you to read the book while all the time providing you as little information as I can manage to get away with.

Kind of the same game the lady with a nice voice plays with you when she waxes eloquent about the premium credit-card you just qualified for, the one with all those nice benefits like cashbacks and frequent flier miles, while conveniently forgetting to divulge information about its high annual fee and its Shylockian APR(Annual Percentage Rate).

However, since I am taking the high road over the credit card saleslady here, I feel I do need to tell you a little bit more about the chapters to follow. In the course of the book, I shall try to establish certain theses. For example:

- Indian politicians are misunderstood, selfless patriots.
- Indian wedding ceremonies keep down the divorce rate.
- 'Gunda', a movie made in 1998, was the greatest celluloid creation of Bollywood.
- The heart of India lies in the embodiments of subaltern culture: namely Bhojpuri songs and Mithun-da flicks.
- There are some underlying principles behind the success of Hindi mega-soaps and Indian reality shows, principles even mortals can understand.
- You can start your own management institute.
- Hindi movies taught me how to lead my life.

Now I really have to stop because if I say any more right here, this 'introduction' chapter would have lost its focus.

Which I have been told is bad writing.

A word (actually a bit more than) about the style. This book is not a work of fact nor is it a work of fiction. If you are looking for a single 'story', there is none. Instead there are a number of fairly independent chapters with the only unifying theme running through them being the vehicle of narration – humour and sarcasm.

Throughout this book and throughout my life I have had no intention of offending anyone. If I have unknowingly done so here, I apologize wholeheartedly. Please consider it as a joke that went too far. Kindly excuse.

Even after that, if you do feel the urge to burn this book, kindly do it under expert supervision. Please also try not to make a flaming mess on the streets. If you decide on other forms of protest (like sending me coloured underwear), kindly do have the courtesy to inform me beforehand so that we may be both present and share the media coverage.

In passing, I do have a regret. Coming from the world of blogging, which is an activity critically dependent on interactive user participation through feedback and comments, a book is somewhat restrictive – a one-way street with one person doing the talking and the other doing all the listening.

An experience somewhat like having a conversation with my mother.

This brings me to the problem. I do not know who you are. Are you one of those rare souls who have actually paid money for this book? If you are, was it to read it or to give your seven-month-old something to tear and play around with so that he/she does not damage something actually valuable?

Or are you a friend/relative who has been emotionally blackmailed to leaf through the pages? Or did you get this book as a gift, from a friend you don't particularly like and are thinking of that distant cousin who you, in turn, can gift this book to?

I wish I knew.

I also wish for something else. And that is reader feedback. Of course, there is some feedback you get from your publisher like 'No one is buying your book'. That's valuable. There are other sources of feedback too: like buying samosas and discovering them wrapped in the pages of the book you wrote. That's even more valuable.

However, what I am most interested in is what you, the reader, think about the *issues* covered in the book. This is why I am providing my email (mayihebb@gmail.com) and the address of my blog (http://greatbong.net) so as to actively solicit your opinion.

Okay, that is enough of prevaricating.

On to the main course.

What You Get In This Ishh..Speshial Package

You thought this book was frivolous? No way. There is a PhD thesis here. Sort of.

Phd theses are never short. Trust me. I wrote one. Plus you don't want me to skimp on the details of 'choli ke peeche kya hai', do you?

Terrorists try to scare us. Laugh at them.

No, it's not what you think.

The education business is pretty big. The fun of this is you don't really need to give your customers what they paid for.

How can anything, whether a book or a movie, be a hit without a massive desi wedding? Dhik tana dhik tana.

Hindi soaps, reality shows and news – the quick and the dirty. Breaking it down right here. Nowhere else. Exclusive.

CHAPTER 1

The Great National Terror Strategy

1. Bomb blasts happen in a crowded area of Indian city **X**, bringing death, destruction and mayhem in its wake.
2. Within a few hours, startling revelations are made by the administration, bringing to light facts no one could otherwise have guessed.

   'Obviously, it's a terrorist plot,' police chief Sando Singh observes. 'The way it has been done, attempt was to cause the maximum damage to human life.'

   God damn those terrorists. Just when we think that they would try their best to miminize casualties, they go ahead and do something totally unexpected.
3. Someone in the government lets out a blood-curdling warning to the evil men, so scary that the blood of tigers turns to water (old jungle proverb):

   'The wicked designs of terrorists will be thwarted boldly and their attempts will be foiled.'

   He then changes his galabandh and repeats that statement to another television channel.

4. The Opposition demands the resignation of the government. Government blames the Opposition's time in power for the problem. Both of them, at the same time, entreat the country to 'rise above petty politics' while vigorously poking each other in the eye.

5. Emotions run high. One news channel plays ominous music. Another channel cuts in footage from *Matrix* to make the presentation more 'attractive'.

   A concerned anchor asks a victim of terror 'How does it feel?' as the poor person sits on a hospital bed without a limb. Another anchor hyperventilates in front of the camera 'This live footage is being brought to you exclusive by us and only us.'

6. Anxious relatives are asked to leave as politicians visit the affected area, their chakravyuh cordon of security throwing the administration into a tizzy. With cameras clicking away, the VVIPs announce some compensation for the victims. If you died in a plane, your family gets the most. If you died in a train, a little less. If you died on the road, then maybe you should have been on a plane.

7. Some people ask why politicians have Z and Z+ and Z++ category security while the common people, of whom the politicians are supposed to be the servants, are about as secure as a kitten in a den of cobras. They are told that politicians are representatives of the people. And since we cannot protect all the people, we have to make sure that at least their elected principals are safe and snug. Symbolism and all that.

8. Jhola-carrying activists, while shedding tears for the dead and dying, circulate a petition that blames India for the damage done to its citizens and paint the terrorists as

poor, misunderstood, slightly murderous Robin Hoods.

9. Massive candle-light vigils are held. The metropolis says in one voice 'No more'. Youngsters passionately speak of the need for accountability, change and greater awareness.

10. The Twenty20 tournament begins on Thursday. The topic of 'national security' goes from Page 1 to Page 4.

11. Shahrukh Khan releases his latest blockbuster *Kya Kuch Naheen Hota Hain*. It is a hit. 'National security' now goes from Page 4 to the inside of Page 7, right next to the Obituaries section.

12. People go on with their lives determined to put the past behind them, determined not to let terrorists win. In short, they forget.

13. A man on a false passport near Indian city **Y** dials a number in a certain neighbouring country. He has with him a large number of ball-bearings, a remote control and some ammonium nitrate.

14. **Y** becomes the next **X**.

15. Go to Step 1.

CHAPTER 2

Moro-Cop – The Diary of a Moral Cop

This chapter contains a few pages from the diary of a moro-cop – a unique species of Homo sapiens who labour under the belief that they have been given an extra-constitutional, patriotic mandate to rid the country of influences they consider to be 'morally corrupting'.

A word (actually more than one) about the language used in the diary. Ever since the British took over Hindustan, it was considered a sign of refinement and education (in brief, 'coolness') to be able to 'talk Ingliss and walk Ingliss'. However, by the 2000s, young Indians or as they like to call themselves Youngistan, influenced by similar sentiments in many parts of the world, collectively came to the conclusion that Queen's English, being full of irritating concepts like vowels (which made it difficult to type sentences fast using cellphone keypads) and boring rules of spelling and sentence construction, was no longer suitable as a medium for expressing the myriad thoughts and emotions of today's people...sorry...2dayz ppl.

This led to the growth of a new language[1] namely SMS-ese, a mutation of English whose conscious subversion of the conventions of grammar and the uSe of mixed capitalization like 'dIs' was considered a means to be 'with it' and most importantly express 'aTTiTude'.

The best thing about SMS-ese was that, because of its fundamental focus on individuality, it allowed the interlocutor to use his own style of spelling and sentence construction (as this diarist has done) thus obviating the need for formal education and learning (a concept Youngistan hated with a passion) with the only restriction being that your personalized style of expression had to be 'N-Ur-Face'.

---

1 Keen observers have noted that SMS-ese sometimes had marked similarities with old English like when 'time' was spelt as 'tyme' (e.g. 'But Salomon seith every thyng hath tyme' from *Canterbury Tales*) or when 'It was' was abbreviated as 'Twas' (e.g. 'So sober fell 'twas wonderful to see' again from *Canterbury Tales*, written at the end of the fourteenth century)

JANUARY 30

Log N2 ma Orkut accnt. Thru the
sunny day, Net connaction is sitty sitty. → *possibly means 'shitty shitty'*
2 nu pix to my album I did upload.

Both of them my boy frans tell me is
ROKING. By the way, word 'frans' is   *we think the diarist is trying*
not Ne longer fashion. Nstead 2 uz → *to say homeboys*
'homoboys' coz it sounds more hop. → *possibly means hip*

   Pix let me describe. One of deez
pix has me with a bare chest & a red
goggle. At my bottom says MiSTer → *possibly means caption*
HOT OR sIR KOOL. Da other 1 has
me pumping my mussels and that is → *muscles and not the seafood,*
bottomed as 'deSHinG dAVil w8Ing   *possibly*
for U'.   *'waiting'*

   But me not just macho like Sanal → *arguably a typo*
Shitty. Me also sansative. 2 show dat,   *this is supposed to mean 'rose'.*
I have also uploaded pix of a baby   *If you look from the right and*
kissing another baby and a lil gal with   *turn your head, it looks like*
a @};-   *a rose. Kind of.*

JANUARY 31

Set my relationship status as
'open relationship'. Dats open 4
relationship.

FEBRUARY 1

2day is da day. I sent many massages
of fransip 2 many 'HOT bAbES'. Hope → *the next stage of 'friendship'*
sum becum labhsip.   *being 'loveship'*

FEBRUARY 3

understand	I do not undrst& dis. Not undrst&
	at all. Deez bAbES, every 1 of them,
an action in a social	have said no 2 my fransip offer. Most
networking site by which one	have put iggy on me. One gal, Sharmi,
blocks persistent friendship	wrote 'fuG off loser'. Pretty told 'nO
seekers	inTrst, hv manE frans'. Y such they
a bit of Yoda	wrote. I know not.

FEBRUARY 5

One reply. Yas. Da girlie cutie tells me
2 meet @Barrista 4 fransip. I am so
heppy. She not have any pix of her
gud self on her profile. Only picture
of Asin. She must B as beautiful. It
possible.

FEBRUARY 6

a disassociative experience	Met her @Barrista. Twas not she. Twas
wherein the diarist still	he. I asked her Y she break my heart.
wants to believe it is a 'she'.	He told me dat he had done so with
perhaps meant 'intent'	good desire. His name is Raghusree
	& he runs organization called 'Pavitra
What the prophets of today	Vahini'. He Bcums girls 2 save boyz like
have to do to get followers.	me, so dat he can meet us and show
They have to pretend to be	us the true light of our dharma and
girls. Moses never had it this	our old history.
tough	

FEBRUARY 8

Met Raghu-sir & 4 first time he make
my eye open. He take me 2 a disco & *perhaps figuratively*
showed me all babes going in. Their
cloths were short. Raghu-sir tells me
dat deez gals will not reply to my
fransip offer because my Ingliss not so
gud and me not have ny car. Day I have
a car dey will run 2 to me. Raghu-sir said
I am very hansome. He said I am chimp. → *we think he means 'champ'*
  My mother also agree.
  Raghu-sir said dey will not cum coz → *I think the diarist missed a*
they not remembr our kulchur Dey *'to me' after the come*
always say 'no' 2 good Indian boy like → *means culture*
myself. Dey always like importd stuffs
and boyz hu have no kulchur. Raghu-
sir sez that we need 2 save da gals.
2morrow dey will bcum our mothers
& sisters & our wives. They will do
Western things, teach bad things 2
small kiddies and do divorce and go
discing with other man like they do in
USA. Dis not Indian. Stop Dis.
  As the song from old Dev Anand
phillum go:
  'Man ko dhakle gori tan ka dhakna
hai bekar Phool na mehke jab tak uska
khilna hai bekar.'
  Look thru more albums of gals.
Such small dressy. 2 saxy. Sent five
more fransip offers.

FEBRUARY 9

Five more ignores on Orkut.

FEBRUARY 10

2day Raghu-sir took me n 4 other boys 2 a park. He said 2 us 'Look'. Such shameless boyz n gals putting hand here there. Dis is not Indian kulchur. Dis like having food in front of hungry beggar. Raghu-sir told us we will have to stop dis akraman on our sabhyata.

a rare moment of honesty attack and civilization

He told us dat on February 14 on Bhelentine's Day we will take 2 streets and stop dis nuisance.

FEBRUARY 11

FeelN sad. When will I have gud Indian gal for Bhelentine?

FEBRUARY 14

Day of action. In morning, 5 of us catch guy n gal holdin hand in pubic. Not gud. Decent Indian boy like me hold themselves b4 marriage. Not gal hand. Raghu-sir take tar from road work and put it on boyz face. Then we make boy and gal get marry in street. Kulchur save.

pubic is possibly a typo

I am sure the double meaning behind this line was not intentional

In noon, we phi8 in front of card shop. Raghu-sir tell me dis is like

we think this means 'fight'

freedom straggle where dey burn
phoren cloths. 2day I smash window
of card shop, break 5 musical cards. I   *not only does he not know*
also set fyre 2 pink teddy bear n burst   *the spelling of fighter, he also*
7 balloons shape like heart. 2day I feel   *does not know the meaning*
like freedom father.   *of freedom*

   In evening, we went 2 disc. Stood
outside and shout shout. More gals
came in small cloths. Then vid cameras
came from nude channels. Raghu-sir   *we do not know if this is a*
made speech about sanskriti, sabhyata   *Freudian slip in the context*
and naari. Then we attack boyz n gals.   *of the 'girls in small clothes'*
Me go after 1 boy hu driving a Corolla.
I /his tire and break car window. I do   *means 'slash'*
not have such a car. 2day dat boy does
not have car also. Then I slap the boy.
Also punch. He have. I just have not.
Not fair. Not Indian.

FEBRUARY 15

Raghu-sir is on all newspaper. I like
him. Elections coming. I will work for
Pavitra Vahini.

FEBRUARY 16

Look through more Orkut profiles. So
many hoT hunnies. So many baBes to
save. So many fransip to make.
   So leetel opportunity.
   Jai sanskriti mata.

There has been a disease that has attained pandemic proportions in India. Competitive intolerance. Every group in India (cultural, religious, regional, you name it) is engaged in a race to get offended.

Something has offended you. Okay. I am going to be offended by something even more trivial. Beat that!

Now if people lay down on the ground and wailed like little babies every time they got offended then it would not be such a big problem. However, what we see becoming the norm is for people to show their hurt and anguish in increasingly spectacular ways (burning of flags, riots, public interest litigations, demands for bans). This is why you have to be very careful nowadays lest something you say sets in motion a chain of events that culminates in you landing up in jail or having your head being hoisted on the end of a spear.

This is why I have compiled a table of 'offensive' words and their 'inoffensive' counterparts. I do so as a public service in the hope we have a gentler, kinder and more understanding world.

Barber: Hairdresser
Tailor: Fashion designer
Grocer: Food retailer
Pickpocket: Economic offender
Bank robber: Investment banker
Snake oil salesman: Research proposal writer
Bonded slave: PhD student
Incorrigible gossip: Blogger
Mujra: Item number
Copying: Internalising
Spousal Abuse: S&M

Terrorist: Misguided youth
Wife/Husband: Partner
Partner: Business associate
Sleeping partner: Financier
Casting couch: Talent show
Pakistan: Frontline ally in the war on terror
Leching: Aggressively appreciating
Fat: Healthy
Bombay: Mumbai
Criminal: Politician
Scary-looking woman: Woman of high moral character
Ugly-looking man: Bachelor of engineering
Code coolie: Software engineer

CHAPTER 3

Nowhere Resident Indians

A strange species the NRI is – one that never fails to evoke strong emotions, be they be of derision, mockery, adulation or professed indifference.

Non-resident Indian? Non-required Indian?

Is he a patriot who by staying outside the country reduces the nation's carbon footprint, relaxes the load on its strained infrastructure and contributes to the GDP by sending money to the homeland by Western Union every month?

Or is he a dollar/euro/dinar-sprouting vision of evil that reneges on his pledge to serve the homeland? The kind that when he comes back to India keeps muttering in his faux accent, 'Aww such poverty. So dirty. Oooh aah.'

Who exactly are these people?

Should we worship the ground they stand on? Or hate them with a passion?

Let's first turn to Bollywood, that glamorous overlord that influences the way we Indians dress, the way we talk, the way we romance – hell whom am I kidding? The way we do virtually everything.

Well, what does it have to say about the NRIs?

According to the movie moguls, there are several kinds of them.

THE SENIOR UBER PATRIOTS

If you tear open the chest of any NRI who belongs to this category, you will find Bharat Mata, with a green card in her hand, standing there.

Even though he may have immigrated away to faraway places like the US and the UK for economic opportunities, the senior uber patriot can still smell the earthy fragrance of home in the morning, more so when he has had red chilli and sarson da saag the night before. Not just that, while feeding the pigeons at Trafalgar Square, he hopes to find a desi bird among them. He still speaks English with a very heavy Indian accent and whenever he meets a desi freshly arrived from the motherland asks:

'Kya ab bhi wahan rajarani ke kisse dadi sunati hai?

Kya ab bhi wahan par bachhon ko maa lori ga ke sulati hai'[1]

English translation:

Do the grandmas there (i.e., back in the homeland) still tell stories of kings and queens? Do the mothers still sing lullabies to the little ones to put them to sleep?

[Needless to say, the freshly arrived Indian smiles sanguinely and nods his head in affirmation, if for nothing else than to not

---

[1] From the song 'Ooh Yaaron Maaf Karna' in *Aa Ab Laut Chalen*.

break the NRI's romantic image of the homeland. The truth is grandma back home couldn't care a rat's ass about tales of kings and queens and is instead devouring stories of extramarital affairs and illegitimate kids on afternoon soaps. And lullaby-singing mother is at kitty parties watching *Desperate Housewives* on DVD while the little one is on the Net, watching Mallika Sherawat kiss Emran Hashmi with wet lips. Nothing wrong in keeping up appearances however.]

Even amidst the moral decrepitude of the West, the uber patriot maintains his sanskriti and maryada. That means he still goes to the temple, is outraged by Pamela Anderson (though he does watch *Baywatch* for its gripping stories) and considers weepie superstar Nirupa Roy, as opposed to Aishwarya Rai, a role model. And finally, at the drop of a hat, he can break into:

London dekha Paris dekha aur dekha Japan
Michael dekha Elvis dekha sab dekha meri jaan
Sare jag mein kahin nahin hai doosra Hindustan
Yeh duniya ik dulhan
Dulhan ke mathe ki bindiya
Yeh mera India I love my India
Watan mera India sajan mera India
Dharam mera India

[English translation: I have seen London, Paris. I have even seen Japan. I have seen Michael (Jackson) and I have seen Elvis (Presley). My dear, I have seen everything. But nowhere in the world is there a second India. If the world is a bride, then India is the red dot on its forehead. This is my India. I love her. My land is India. My lover is India. My religion is India]

And the most amazing thing is that even after singing the above encomiums for the watan in which the word 'India' occurs six times in succession, he chooses to reside in London, Paris and sometimes even Japan.

THE SECOND-GENERATION CULTURAL REPROBATE

If you meet a member of this tribe and if that member be a male of the species, then be prepared to encounter someone who fits the following stereotype: a faux American/British accent with a profusion of 'Yo man's' and 'Come baby come baby's', a baseball cap, a fast car without a hood and, most tellingly, a healthy disregard for Indian culture that includes disrespect for elders. Oh how can I forget – a 'white' girlfriend who dresses too provocatively.

And if it be a girl, you will see her smoking and drinking (Hindi movie: vamp alert) and also dressed in clothes that mothers and sisters should not try on. While out to snare the bhola bhala simple Indian from the homeland, she makes no secret of her wanton ways, which includes cavorting around in strip clubs watching girls dance. (Yes, you heard that right. If you do not believe me, I ask you to look at the second stanza of the song 'O tashi anata' from *Aa Ab Laut Chalen* where the Suman Ranganthan-NRI-character is shown doing precisely that, much to the disgust of her 'pure Indian' beau played by Akshaye Khanna.)

These characters are, however, not often beyond redemption. For example, a male specimen of this kind may be rescued from the abyss of moral decimation by an ever-sacrificing, innocent woman from the homeland in whose laughter you find the ethereal rhythm of spring water from the Gangotri (and who is helpfully called 'Ganga'). Through her steadfast devotion to culture, her singing of slow melodious songs in a Lata Mangeshkarian voice, and her standing by his side after he suffers an accident while driving his Mustang over the bridge, she has the power to turn the NRI over to what *Star Wars* fans would call the light side of the force. However, this does not happen to all, and some, unable to 'rise in love', are removed from the story, defeated, in the last reel (the Apoorva Agnihotri character in *Pardes*, for example. The fact that he was in competition with Shahrukh Khan for the attention of Ganga – Mahima Chowdhury – didn't make things any easier, of course.]

THE IDEAL SECOND-GENERATION NRI

If a few of you are shaking your heads by now, disgusted at this twisted depiction of second-generation Indians, fikar not.

Not all of them are cultural reprobates. No,not at all. There is something called the good pardesi. Even though these people may ride helicopters into their palace garages and dance to 'Kehdo na you are my soniya' in lock-step with skimpily clad mems (phoren ladies) at discos, these worthies have their hearts and heads firmly in place. In other words, when push comes to shove, trust them to dive eagerly into gaajar ka halwa prepared by dadima (abandoning burger and fries) while moving their heads, full of devotion, to desi bhajans.

Overall, however, it must be said that the portrayal of NRIs by Bollywood is very sympathetic. Obviously the fact that the 'overseas' market is one of the biggest catchment areas for Bollywood movies and stage shows has nothing to do with it.

Having stayed outside the country for a few years, I have formed my own idea of these NRI people, based on my interactions with them at desi parties.

A caveat. Being a Bengali myself, my social circle consists almost exclusively of Bengali NRIs. Hence the stereotypes

I present may have more than a bit of Bengali bias in them. Kindly excuse.

Setting: An NRI party. This is usually organized in a school, rented on a Saturday evening. There is typically a religious reason for the gathering – for us Bongs, it is usually Durga and Saraswati Puja.

Let us imagine us, you and me, transmogrified into two flies. We are buzzing about, listening to scraps of conversation, studying people, taking a lick off the rosogollas on the aluminium tray every once in a while and doing that thing we desis most love to do – judging others.

THE DISTINGUISHED ELDERLY GENT

He is almost always found wearing a suit on 'formal occasions'- which means any time he is invited anywhere. He is proud of the fact that he still wears a housecoat at home. He smokes a pipe, likes English Earl Grey tea and always sips it thinking of the queen. He never tires of reminding people that his granddad was a Rai Bahadur (a honorary title given to people who had sufficiently wetted with saliva the boots of the British) and how India would have been a 'Number 1 country', as opposed to the 'third world hellhole' it is today, had the British still stayed on.

He forgets to mention that he is descended from the 'dancing [nautch] girl' side of the Rai Bahadur family. He also does not like to accept that the loss of his brain has not affected India as much as he likes to believe.

He will barge into conversations with stories of how he arrived in the USA with only eight dollars in cash, and how his generation had it so tough in comparison with today's tykes.

And whatever you do, do not refer to him as simply Mr Sen or Mr Gupta if he holds a PhD or is an MBBS. It is 'Doctor' Sen or 'Doctor' Gupta. If you do address him as 'Mr', or worse, by his first name, be prepared for a red angry stare that would make Churchill shake in his boots, and an accompanying crackle of 'insolent brat'.

THE DESI AUNTY TYPE I

She is immensely proud of her offspring(s). That in itself is fine – even my mother is proud of me, so I am hardly in a position to judge others in that respect. But what distinguishes the Desi Aunty Type I from the other mothers of the world is that her main reason for being at the party is to steer all conversation to the topic of her super-achieving son/daughter in the same manner that, within a minute, any conversation between two teenage boys turns to oversized mammaries.

Example snippet

Lady 1: Ms Banerjee, what is happening to our country? So many terrorist attacks – things were not as bad as this when we were in India. No?

Desi Aunty Type I: What to say! I am always telling my husband what a good thing it is we got green card and have settled down here. I was also saying this to my son yesterday evening when he called me from his dorm in Stanford. You know he is there on a President's fellowship? His dad wanted him to go to MIT because MIT was also giving him a fellowship and it would be closer home. But my son said he liked the weather in California! What to do – today's children.

Another example snippet

Lady 1: It's been years since I have been to an Association get-together. My knee has been giving so much trouble. It's so difficult to get a good doctor here with all the insurance hassles...

Desi Aunty Type I: Thankfully I don't have such a problem. I don't know if you know but my daughter is doing her residency in Johns Hopkins. Whenever I even so much as sneeze, she is at my place in an instant, and no matter how many times I say 'I am fine' she will take me to the best doctors at Hopkins. They all see me, without any charge. They keep telling me, 'Aunty, your daughter is the best doctor we have at Hopkins. We need to give you the best treatment so that we can stay on her good side.'

The fun however is when the conversation is between two ladies of Desi Aunty Type I. This is when the game of one-upmanship begins, where it is as much about whose offspring is professionally better off as it is of showing how, despite being so busy and so rich, laadli always has her parents in her thoughts.

Desi Aunty Type I Specimen 1: I forgot to tell you last time but Reshmi got a very good modelling offer from a jeweller's in New Jersey. She really wanted to do this as the pay was really good, and to make things even more embarrassing, the people from the modelling agency were literally camping outside our house. But Dr Sen just would not relent (lowering voice). In any case, she has started medical school and I am sure she will get many such opportunities in the future...

Desi Aunty Type I Specimen 2: Dr Sen is right, you know. My baby Priya was approached a year ago, just when she turned twenty, by a top Bollywood director – you know, the one who made *Humare Woh Aapke Haath Mein Hai*. He wanted to cast her in his next production opposite Ran-tham-bore Kapoor. Can you imagine that? No auditions... nothing. But Priya turned it down straightaway – she did not even ask us. Proper upbringing, you know! As it is, good thing she did, considering that at twenty-two she is already partner in law firm of Kapoor, Kapoor, Kapoor and Kapoor located on M street, Washington DC.

THE DESI AUNTY TYPE II

Very similar to Desi Aunty Type I. As opposed to offspring, her source of pride comes from her wealth, her jewellery, her house, her cars, her saris and the material largesse of immigranthood. And she does not hesitate to flaunt it or rub it in, when and if she is in the mood. Which is nearly always.

Lady 1: At last we bought a house. I am so looking forward to moving out of our rented apartment.

Desi Aunty Type II: So where did you buy this house?

Lady 1: Randolph Road.

Desi Aunty Type II: Oh my! Have you already paid for it?

Lady 1: Y-yes.

Desi Aunty Type II: That is such an unsafe place. Not a good place to raise a daughter, let me tell you. Of course I understand that houses are cheap there but really that's such a run-down part of the town. Much better Elf Green where we stay. But of course even the smallest lots there start at half a million. (Sympathetic stare.)

Another example

Desi Aunty Type II Specimen 1: Our India trip this time went by so quickly. I spent all my time getting some necklaces and earrings made. The price of gold nowadays – oh my. Five years ago, when I last went to India, I bought double this amount and it cost half as much. And the craftsmanship – it's not quarter as good as it is used to be. But it is still better than the gold here in the US – you cannot get more than 18 carats.

Desi Aunty Type II Specimen 2: That's because you don't know the right places. I have this person who gets all my stuff imported from India. Have to tell you – the stuff is exclusive. Look at this necklace. Of course this perhaps costs double what you paid even this time in India but the difference in workmanship between yours and mine makes it worth the extra premium.

Desi Aunty Type II Specimen 1: Well I would rather save the extra premium and spend it on diamonds. As my daughter says, 'Gold is so auntyish.' (Exchange of poisonous stares). I prefer to keep up with the times.

Yet another example

Desi Aunty Type II to her friends: Did you hear Mrs Banerjee is now working ever since her husband got laid off?

Friends: Where?

Desi Aunty Type II: At the checkout counter of a dollar store. It is so sad. I was walking past the store and our eyes met. The poor lady just looked away in shame.

Friends: Yes, so very sad.

THE PYRAMID SCHEME UNCLE

The friendliest people in a desi party, these are by far the most dangerous. Insidious denizens of evil with a friendly smile on their faces, they will spot a person standing in a corner and quietly slip beside him and strike up a conversation. Their aim: to recruit the unsuspecting into their army of undead amateur vampires so that they in turn may bite and infect other innocents with ruinous 'get rich quick' schemes, in the process creating an ever-increasing army of pure darkness.

Let me explain how this works.

A kindly man, in his mid-forties, approaches you at the party. Unlike the other snobs and the elites who will impose themselves and keep blabbering about how great they are, this guy actually expresses an interest in you – what do you do, where do you live, and most importantly, what your phone number is. (This is like the vampire searching for your neck – only you do not know it yet.) Whatever you say, he shows himself to be impressed.

Then he slips in the first question.

'Are you satisfied with your present income?'

This is of course a question whose answer is obvious. No one is satisfied with their current income. Just like their sex life.

You say no.

This is of course your first big mistake. It is like throwing away the garlic and the cross when a caped man with fangs is standing in front of you.

He then tells you of a marvellous business that he and his friends are involved in. They usually do not let people into their exalted circle but they can always make an exception for an intelligent, educated and motivated person like yourself.

You feel intrigued and perhaps even a bit flattered.

Second big mistake. Now one foot of yours is already in the coffin.

You ask about the nature of the business. He is strangely evasive. When you press on, he will make you believe it is as complicated as the General Theory of Relativity. As you stare at him blankly, he will assure you that it will all become clear once you visit him at his place.

Right around this time, you are perhaps feeling a little doubtful. So you try to worm your way out of this engagement by either saying 'I do not have time right now' or 'I do not own a car'.

He will be very accommodating. If time is your problem, he will say it will only be a few minutes. If it is the lack of conveyance, he will volunteer to pick you up himself and drop you off. He will even offer dinner.

So insistent is he in his good-naturedness, you just have to say yes. After all, you do not want to offend such a polite fellow.

Third and final mistake. You have now officially stepped into the coffin and the vampire is polishing his fangs.

So a week later you are at his house. While he will possibly not, in the fashion of Lord Dracula, say 'Welcome Mr Harker, please leave behind some of the happiness you bring,' he will be very glad to see you.

He will offer you bhujia and tea. Yes that's dinner. Maybe a Diet Coke. Then the scheme will be unveiled, like the proverbial denouement at the end of an Agatha Christie novel.

Except here you are the victim.

The plan is simple. You sell this company's amazing products

– beauty bars, toothpaste, perfumes, garden implements, any and everything to your 'contacts'. For every sale, you get a slice of the revenue. However, the main moneymaker is when you get other people to sign on to the franchise. For every new person you bite – sorry, convince – to sign up in this scheme, you get a share of his commissions. Technically this is called a pyramid scheme and it is used, in addition to vampires, by zombies and werewolves.

You have now two options. You can jump into the coffin and close the lid. In other words, join the scheme and become a footsoldier in the army of the undead.

The other option is to say, 'No thank you.'

Well, if you take this fork in the road, be prepared for an incessant barrage of hardsell, emotional blackmail, and insistent calls at home (remember they asked for your phone number) till you have to do that thing you were so afraid of doing weeks ago.

Act rude.

The Sari Vending Aunty

Very similar to Pyramid Scheme Uncle, her modus operandi is slightly different. She doesn't slip in beside the first prey she finds. Instead she waits till she builds up an extensive circle of aunty friends. And then one fine day, at a kitty party or at a desi occasion, she unleashes on the unsuspecting world her collection of overpriced saris, cut out from the same cloth used to make Govinda's costumes in *Coolie Number 1*. This is accompanied by – yes you guessed it – hardsell ('Buy one, just one, it looks so good on you'), peer pressure ('Kavita-didi bought two, Meena bought three, your husband just got promoted to project manager, let me write you down for two at least'), and emotional blackmail ('If you buy one, you are my friend. If you do not, you are not.' Kind of like George W. Bush's 'You are either with us or against us').

The fun is magnified if Sari Vending Aunty is also a member of Desi Aunty Type II clan. If she is, she will sell you her factory-reject saris, make a tidy profit, use the money to buy a good sari or two herself and then patronizingly tell you 'Wow, you look so good in that sari' with a smug, satisfied smile greasing the pudgy cheeks, crying out noiselessly: Loser loser.'

THE CAUSE-ESPOUSING DADA

As the cliché goes: You can take a man out of India but you cannot take India out of a man. Neither fortunately can you exorcize the politics out of him. Even though technically the last time he cast his vote in an Indian elections was when Indira Gandhi won in Chikmagalur and even though he is a permanent resident/citizen in a foreign country, you would be forgiven for thinking that he just came to the party from a political procession, so fired up are his eyes and so much dry froth accumulated in the corner of his lips.

Okay, I exaggerate. Most Cause-espousing Dadas are easygoing, agreeable people with vaselined unchapped lips and the smell of fresh talcum powder, who just happen to have a strong political streak in them. And like the previously mentioned Type I aunties, they exhibit a marked predilection for steering almost every conversation to their pet political themes. Within the blink of an eye.

Gentleman 1: Oh I think Rahat Ali Khan's latest CD is simply amazing.

Cause-espousing Dada: I really do not understand why

Pakistani artists are allowed to sell their music in India when our music is banned there. It has to do with our policy of minority appeasement. If only…

Cause-espousing Dadas come in all shapes and forms, reflecting the full spectrum of Indian political opinion.

There is the staunch Gandhian who talks about a new village-centric economic model for India and the virtues of high thinking and clean living. True to his ideals, he is a committed teetotaler (so much so that he refuses to even have rum cake), never raises his voice in an argument, always stands in front of the paneer line leaving the chicken dish for you with a gentle smile, throws his soft drink bottle into the recycle-only bin, drives a fuel-efficient hybrid car, stays in a gated community of eco-friendly, one-million-dollar homes called The Green Village, and has a poster of Mahatma Gandhi in his manager's office at one of the nation's foremost aerospace companies, where he leads a group of two hundred who design fighter planes and enhanced-delivery future combat systems for a secret defence project.

Then there is the ex-Naxalite who escaped in the '70s to the United States, still reminiscing about those golden days when he hid in the paddy fields, running from the tyrannical police, his eyes swelling up with tears as the faces of dead and missing comrades come rushing in. Despite the thirty-five years spent in the Soviet Socialist Republic of New York, everybody agrees that he still has not lost an iota of revolutionary fervour. His inner voice still sings in solidarity with the peasants of Guatemala and cries out silently in protest against the World Bank, the World Trade Organization and other instruments of Western imperialism every waking second – in the bath, on the golf course and even while reclining in his first-class seat on a trans-Atlantic flight as he wonders whether his company should invest in sugarcane futures.

And finally Saffron Hindutva Uncle, whose favourite soccer team is Netherlands because he likes their jerseys, who catches hold of young people in a party and explains to them, in a voice brimming with passion, how the atom bomb was designed during the Mahabharata and how the ancient ones invented the exclamation mark. He then fulminates about sinister conspiracies involving assimilation of the Sanatana culture and rants on about the corrupting influences of various sorts tearing apart the moral fibre of the nation, glancing all the while over his shoulder at imagined enemies out to convert him. He then slips a folder in your hand and asks you to join the 'cause'.

As you try slinking away to another corner of the party, promising to look at the material, you are only too happy when a kindly gentleman rescues you from this uncomfortable situation with a 'Are you satisfied with your income?'

The Cultural Aunty

Singing. Dancing. Elocution.

How can a desi party be complete without some culture?

After all, just talking and bitching does get boring after a while.

Have no fear.

The Culture Aunty is here.

Imagine the following scenario. A group of desis in a living room just talking among themselves. Suddenly, an overtly enthusiastic person will step into the limelight wanting to organize a cultural intervention.

Culture Aunty: Come on, come on Sushimol-da. You have

to sing. Please please. Konika said you sing so well... Please please.

Alternatively...

Culture Aunty: Enough chatter. Let us organize into two teams. Antaskhari antakshari. All the gentleman on one side. No no Uma-didi, no slinking away to the corner...

While the desire to breathe some sort of life into a desi party is no doubt an admirable one, even at the cost of Sushimolda's irritation and Uma-didi's reticence, the motivation behind the alacrity exhibited by the Culture Aunty is somewhat less altruistic than one may think. And what is that motive? Namely that Aunty wants to sing or dance or recite poetry herself and be the cynosure of all eyes but finds it embarrassing to suddenly, out of the blue, take center-stage herself. Hence the elaborate ruse of getting you involved in what is basically an ego-trip.

And so the plan is brought to fruition. As the said Aunty closes her eyes, shakes her head excessively like a freshly decapitated chicken to the music and goes *'Aaaaaa Aaaaa Aaaaaabhhh, she je boner horeen chilo amar mone'* [translated from Bangla to English as 'Aaaaa Aaaaaa Aaaaaaah, the deer from the forest was in my mind], all the while trembling her voice like a bleating spring lamb, the tired veteran of many desi parties endures, with a degree of morbid fascination, this outpouring of culture as he contemplates the truth of what the great philosopher Ralph Waldo Emerson once said: 'Culture, with us, ends in headache.'

THE ANGRY SECOND-GENERATION KID

No sight is as tragic as that of a broken spirit. Well, not quite. No sight but that of a second-generation American born desi teenager slinking away in a corner of a desi party, watching the proceedings with an expression that borders on boredom and hate, alternating between stifled yawns and poisonous glances at the people assembled. Dragged along by overbearing parents in order to get in touch with his roots, either as his side of the bargain to get an increase in allowance or to get his own car to drive, he stands in a stress position, like an enemy combatant in Guantánamo Bay, counting seconds till the torture may end.

Things are not made easy by assorted aunties squeezing his cheeks and saying how much he has grown since the last time they saw him. The only consideration made to his awkwardness is that a couple of pizzas and soda are ordered and kept on another table, separate from the naans and the paneers, as an indulgence to the second generation's palate.

After all this slow torture by culture, don't call the kid 'confused' if he wants to stay as far away from his roots as possible.

THE 'WILL YOU MARRY MY DAUGHTER' AUNTY

If you thought Pyramid Scheme Uncle and Sari Vending Aunty are the only two types of people with things they want to offload in a desi party, then you obviously have not met my 'Will You Marry My Daughter' Aunty. Though they be settled abroad (and perhaps even more so because they are), they want a pure desi son-in-law for their laadli. Afraid that their daughters may get hitched to a wannabe hiphop star with a love for the 'thug' lifestyle or to a guy who drives a pick-up truck and has beer running down the front of his baniyaan, their heart searches for a first-generation desi arrived from the country with their unaccented English, button-up cotton shirts and graduate fellowships, so that they may provide their daughters with cultured stability in the same way that their husbands have provided for them.

So these Aunties slip into the desi parties and their eyes scan the crowd for appropriately innocent-looking FOBs (Fresh Off Boats – the derisive term for recently arrived immigrants). Once the target is locked in, she moves in for the kill.

Of course, she doesn't go up and say 'Will you marry my daughter?'

No. Surely not. That would be a totally uncool move.

What instead she does is start up a conversation in the manner of Pyramid Scheme Uncle. She asks about the FOB's educational qualifications, what his parents do back in India and other vital bits of information in as unobtrusive a manner as possible. Once the checklist in her mind has been completed, she makes the opening move.

Possible Gambit 1: 'Why don't you come and teach my daughter some Bangla? I love the way you have maintained your connection with roots so far from home.'

Possible Gambit 2: 'I am sure you miss home-cooked food. Come over to our house sometime.'

Possible Gambit 3: 'Oh so you know classical music. Please. Why don't you come some day and teach my daughter some...'

Yes. Classical music.

Needless to say, for the FOBs these are direct appeals to the stomach and to the ego, very difficult for anyone to resist. To top it off, an FOB is always vulnerable to a friendly maternal voice in a foreign land, struggling as he is to fit in.

Some FOBs are of course, to quote Britney Spears, 'not that innocent', and catch on to what is being proposed. And it sounds quite good – female company, and that too from an ABCD (American Born Confused Desi being the acronym favoured by the FOB), universally considered hot and desirable, under parental approval, with the not-unpleasant possibility of citizenship through marriage.

But be careful of Greeks bearing gifts.

And even more so of desi aunties with attractive proposals.

Realize that the possibility of the girl turning out to be a Priyanka Chopra lookalike blown away by your knowledge of Cobol programming and Carnatic music is about the same as that of retiring to a mansion in the Bahamas at the age of forty off the income accrued through the pyramid scheme. What is slightly more possible is that once the girl realizes you are not only the parent-approved candidate but also dress and talk like her dad, her entire pent-up aggression of being made to attend desi parties, not being allowed to wear an off-shoulder dress to prom, and being forced to put coconut oil in her hair, will be unleashed on you.

Stay away. Stay very far away.

CHAPTER 4

A Sociocultural Study of Sexual Frustration in India – Back to the Future

Time: Sometime in 2310.

Setting: A classroom. Humans, androids, amdroids, cyborgs, hulcans in attendance.

A holographic image of a professor stands on the lecture podium.

Professor: In today's class, we will start a new topic: A Sociocultural Study of Sexual Frustration in India (From the 1980s to the 2000s) – A Media Perspective. In our last lecture, we looked at the geopolitical implications of the immense frustration that was caused by segregation of sexes in countries of the Middle East. To recap, many men simply blew themselves up because they were convinced that the act of suicide would give them unlimited carnal pleasures in heaven, so hopelessly hopeless was their life on earth.

Now, I realize that in today's age of erotic simulations, artificially implanted memories and pleasure robots, where the necessity for a partner has been eliminated, this is tough for most of you to understand but the world in the age of ignorance (1980s to 2010) was very different from what it is today.

We discussed all these in the last lecture, but to repeat: Mass belief systems called religion as well as prevalent social mores strongly discouraged, to the point of criminalization, carnal contact between individuals who were not bound by ties of a social contract called marriage (as most of you have already taken some sociological history class at the undergraduate level, I am assuming concepts like marriage do not need to be explained in class) particularly in the countries of the Middle East and South East Asia.

Because marriage was sanctioned only after a certain age, people spent a significant portion of their sexually mature life in a state of high emotional anguish, or more precisely in a state of debilitating desperation. In this lecture, our focus will be on male frustration since it had a greater effect on history and on the popular culture of the day than female frustration. We will use the medical term that is commonly used to denote this malaise – Khanna Lahiri Patel Desperation (popularly referred to by its acronym KLPD), named after the scientists who first identified it as a clinical condition.

Please keep all trans-galactic transmitters and auto-pleasuring instruments off during this lecture.

Thank you. Any questions?

Well if there are not, let's continue.

A wealth of authentic archaeological evidence has been unearthed recently that throws much light on the lives of Indian males in the '80s. Confined largely to same-sex educational institutions at the school level by prevalent societal mores, there was very limited scope for interaction with females. Naturally this led to intense frustration among the male population, a maddening sensation that continued for many into their college life, especially for those who opted for engineering studies, which for some strange reason had a systemic paucity of ladies.

The sense of frustration borne out of the lack of opportunities to meet members of the opposite sex was reinforced by the extant media climate. Anthropologists have noted that in properly functioning societies, television and cinema usually step in to provide some release to collective frustration, especially when it threatens to burst open like the gasket of a pressure cooker.

Unfortunately, the media that had the largest reach, namely television, was totally under the control of the government. This meant that its primary purpose was the dissemination of propaganda with stodgy bureaucrats making sure that transmitted programmes were inoffensive as per the moral standards of the day.

To elaborate, there was only one television channel called Doordarshan, abbreviated as DD and controlled by the central government. I am not being facetious when I say it was as far removed from a DD brassiere cup size as possible. DD's mandate was simple. It was to provide to the nation a daily digest of the daily activities of important ministers – at least those that could be shown without shocking the country. What daily activites would these be? The speeches delivered, the ribbons cut, the dignitaries met, the grand initiatives announced.

(Video hologram shows a voice droning on: 'Hamen yeh banana hain, woh banana hain. Desh ko aage badhana hain.')

These daily video communiqués were occasionally interspersed by documentaries on the basket-weavers of Kumaon, serious deliberations on the correct type of seeds to be used for bajra cultivation, white-haired professors teaching techniques of balancing chemical equations by the application of oxidation-reduction method – topics that were no doubt of great significance for the nation but of marginal interest to males in their teens and early twenties looking for some release. This was unless of course you found the laws of refraction or a minister asking countrymen to maintain communal amity to be somewhat arousing.

Android: But professor, what about cinema? As far as I recall, India used to have a vibrant popular cinematic tradition.

Professor: Yes, I am coming to that. You androids always try to get ahead of the discussion. Please desist from such interruptions or I shall be forced to use a circuit-shorting plasma ray. Thank you.

So yes. Leaving aside DD, there was the private film industry. I use the word 'private' to distinguish it from DD which, because it was funded by the State (i.e. taxpayer financed), had no imperative to make money. However, since films were funded by private capital, there were undoubtedly strong motivations to get a significant return on investment. And what easier way to do that than to pander to the basest instincts of the 'starving' population?

However, strict control was sought to be kept on the content of commercial cinema by an entity called the Censor Board of India. Comprising a few random people selected by the government, typically as political favours, they had been given the divine power to purge movies of scenes that were considered to be morally objectionable.

The fact that a non-representative sample of a few humanoids would be given the authority to determine what a few billion people could or could not see might seem to you today to be a bit, for the want of a better word, ludicrous. However, these were the days of extreme ignorance. Remember they still did not know that even male humanoids could be made pregnant under precise temperatures and humidity. Yes, that ignorant.

[Laughter all around except of course from Hulcans, who typically do not show any emotion.]

The job of making sure that the moral fibre of the nation was not ripped to shreds was no easy task. Sitting through hundreds of movie submissions every year, it was the duty of the Censor Board to make sure that a flash of exposed female flesh in improper places was not slipped in between two innocent sequences. The definition of what censors found objectionable ran the gamut of flesh exposure and morally corrupting themes to the depiction of specific political figures in a less-than-flattering light. Scenes were regularly snipped off by censors. Sometimes they banned entire movies.

And yet, despite the draconian controls, titillation would still seep through as long as it satisfied the 'conventions'. For instance, the hero could have pre-marital interactions of the intimate kind with the heroine *only if it was necessary to save her life*. A common plot device of those days was to make the heroine fall through ice and for the hero to engage in sexual congress with her in order to save her from hypothermia (*Ganga Jamuna Saraswati, Aa Gale Lag Ja*). We do not have conclusive proof whether this was a common occurrence in India at that time and to be honest that is not important in this context. What is beyond doubt is that this was significant in terms of the message it conveyed – sex outside marriage was a horrible sin but acceptable only under extenuating circumstances like when body heat became vital for survival.

Among other conventions, vamps or female villains were typically given greater lassitude in terms of the amount of skin exposure they were allowed. This again sent a message: your virtue is inversely proportional to the amount of skin you show. Mind you this show of skin was extremely limited, more precisely limited to what scientists like Khanna, Lahiri and Patel (the KLPD guys) would call a 'peek-a-boo' type of exposure i.e. just enough to get the audience into the unlit theatres but not enough to attract the ire of the nation's keepers of morality.

One of the conventions which has attracted the attention of researchers like Dr Mandakini Ganga has been the use of water as a means for titillation. While the depiction of an unclad female figure was a no-no for the Censor Board, they did not object if the heroine was drenched in water while wearing diaphanous fabrics. This according to Dr Ganga was a compromise, in the best traditions of the Indian concept of 'understanding', an embodiment of the spirit that kept often antagonistic religious and social groups together as one nation. While the censors recognized the needs of moviemakers to recover their investment by showing what the audience wanted, they also were responsible for making sure that poisonous Western ideas like total female nudity did not sully the nation's youth.

The 'wet sari' or the 'Mandakini' effect, as it is called, after the great social scientist, was a beautiful solution acceptable to both. The covering was there but then again it was not there. It was somewhat the metaphor of the 'Indian dream' in the '80s – the object of their aspirations lay in front of them, hidden behind the flimsiest of obstacles. It teased, it tempted. However, it never revealed itself fully, it never seemed attainable, always behind a wet patina of fibre or the transparent but impenetrable wall of red-tape and government control. Needless to say it sent generations of men into deeper stages of KLPD-ness as they were visually stimulated but denied the chance of any kind of release, deprived as they were of any opportunity to consummate the tidal waves unleashed inside them.

However, the Mandakini effect was a blessing from heaven for the movie financers. Going by the adage that once you got them by the gonads the wallet follows, directors would weave in rain, waterfalls, rivers and other aquatic sources into their plots, often at multiple points, leading to the wastage of much water – a fact that may have contributed in no small way to the water riots of the 2050s that were caused by acute water shortages in north India.

Amdroid: So professor, this KLPD-ness seems to be somewhat like, to use a metaphor from the Age of Ignorance, putting the key into the ignition, starting the engine but then never driving the car.

Professor: Yes, somewhat.

Amdroid: As a mechanical being myself, I understand this would be most painful.

Professor: Movie producers also realized that one of the things that the frustrated audiences appreciated were sexually explicit so-called naughty songs. In the 2100s, Dr Sameer sought to explain their inherent appeal by reasoning that verbalizing frustration often serves as a release for pent-up desires.

But moviemakers could not just insert vulgar songs into their products in a random, thoughtless fashion. Here also they had to abide by the conventions of the Censor Board.

This led to the birth of the double-meaning song – verses set to music that had multiple interpretations of which one was innocent and the other was not.

Now this was indeed a tough balancing act. If the hidden meaning was too subtle, then its purpose would be defeated. If the intended meaning was too overt, the censors would refuse to pass it.

This led to another kind of peek-a-boo effect where an apparently innocent juxtaposition of words, when heard in the proper frame of mind, would allude to lewd wantonness.

Let me explain this with two examples culled from the 1980s. Each of these songs and the accompanying visuals have been loaded into the course memory chip and you are now encouraged to watch it.

The first song is from the movie *Mard* (Man) and the words go thus: 'Hum to tamboo mein bamboo lagaye baithe.' Translated into English it means: 'I have poked my bamboo in the tent.' Now whether this song merely expresses the experiences of a character out on a camping trip pitching a tent or whether it signifies a state of humanoid arousal, I leave as an exercise. If you think it is the first choice, just think A. Else B. The telepathy machine will tabulate your answers.

The second song is from the movie *Jadugar* (Magician). Here the lyrics are: 'Padosan apni murgi ko rakhna sambhaal, mera murga hooya hain deewana.' Again the translation, as you can see on your hologram screens, is: 'Neighbour lady, please take care of your hen, my cock is wild.' Anyone who thinks this song refers to a dispute between neighbours over a farm animal is asked to leave the class and put their head in the laser incinerator.

Before we move on to the '90s, I would like to touch upon an interesting sidelight that has recently been the subject of some academic dispute. That is, regarding the role of 'film festivals' as a partial cure for KLPD-ness in metro cities. A famous Kolkata-based commentator of those days, a certain Nitai Chandra Sarkar, wrote a monograph on the popularity of film festivals in major cities, particularly in Kolkata.

While the prevalent opinion was that this fondness for cerebral cinema was due to the intellectual climate that prevailed in the cities, some other researchers, Mr Sarkar being one of them, have provided an alternative, rather surprising, explanation. They propose that the interest in film festivals, or rather, the mad rush for tickets, was in no small measure due to the fact that most of the foreign movies that were shown were uncensored. To support their hypothesis, they provide statistics that show an unusually high interest in movies from the Nordic countries, especially Sweden – countries whose cinematic creations were laxer in general with regard to displaying nudity and other adult activities.

Humanoid: So that's it? The only way for Indians to see uncensored sensual scenes was through film festivals? Since film festival attendance was an exclusive prerogative of the privileged, I can safely assume this was yet one more example of financial deprivation extending to other forms of deprivation in India. Am I correct, Professor?

Professor: Not really. As typically found in cultures where there is repression, the subaltern classes devised their own methods of solving the KLPD problem. Their methods, though technically not legal, were nevertheless extremely prevalent in the inner cities and the suburbs.

The '80s were noted for the proliferation of 'video bars' in small Indian towns. Run principally on private capital provided by local toughs and political power-players (which explains why local law-enforcement officials, by and large, turned a blind eye to their existence), video bars showed illegally smuggled in video cassettes of risqué movies. The typical video bar infrastructure consisted of a darkened back room with a seating capacity of about fifteen, a small-screen television and a video cassette player. There was a bouncer outside the door whose role it was to check that the audience inside had paid their dues and did not engage in unruly and unhygienic behaviour (indiscriminate dissemination of bio-fluids being sometimes a concern). Most importantly, he had to act as a lookout in the rare event that there was a police raid and to 'sort out' matters afterwards.

In larger cities and suburban areas, in addition to video bars there was also a circuit of sleazy theatres which ran uncensored movies in a clandestine way. What was unique about these theatres was that the 'Now Playing' sign outside would be of a 'legal' movie – typically an extremely innocent and old one, so old and innocent that one would wonder why a band of men were standing in line, looking over their shoulders surreptitiously, buying tickets when they could easily stay at home and watch it for free on DD.

Once inside, the film would play as advertised. Except that every few minutes the narrative would be interrupted by scenes from other movies – scenes that, obvious to say, had no connection to the original being shown. This technique was known as 'punching' and has been recognized by cultural historians as yet another insidious device to alleviate the KLPD malaise while keeping the trappings of propriety intact.

A fascinating first-person account of this 'punching' phenomenon can be found in the famous *Diaries of Poltu*, which as all of us know is a fourteen-volume tome written by a teenager named Poltu in the late 1980s and early '90s. This is one of the very few historically accurate descriptions of life that have survived from the metropolis of Kolkata after the destruction wrought by the Great One-Year Bandh of 2034, a year-long self-imposed strike in which the city mysteriously starved itself in order to prevent industrialization of the state. I will be now reading what Poltu writes about his first experience of going to see a 'punched' movie.

It was late afternoon as I made my way to the theatre. My heart had been beating fast ever since I had gotten down from the bus. I was in this really bad part of town, when I should be at the residence of my Physics tutor solving problems on thermal conduction. To make matters even more obvious I was in my school uniform, with my school bag, and on top of that was dragging along an embarrassingly ugly yellow lemon-shaped water bottle filled with boiled water, something my mother insisted I carry. If anyone saw me here and ratted me out to my dad, I would be in a world of hurt. And yet here I was – throwing all caution to the winds, drawn by a force I felt but little understood.

The hall was a dilapidated old building which must have been there from the 1920s. Its walls were stained with human urine, dried dung cakes, political graffiti and paper flyers of various movies. It had one entrance: an arch that had seen better times. Probably during the Non-Cooperation Movement. There was one small window to its side which I assumed to be the box office.

Outside was a sign which gave the name of the movie that was running: Charlie Chaplin's *City Lights*.

Charlie Chaplin indeed!

I approached the box office careful not to make eye-contact with the people milling around the gate, almost all of whom seemed to be the proverbial 'bad men' I had been warned about all my life, the ones who wore just baniyans and smelled of sweat, desi liquor and violence. But then today, I was also like them. I too was 'bad'. Now if only I could lose this yellow water bottle.

With my heart beating out of fear and excitement, I stood in front of the window. There was only one person standing in front of me. He handed Rs 5 to the man inside. No ticket was handed back.

I was now at the front of the line.

A very rough-looking man with an ugly scar that ran down from his temple to his cheek stared back from the dark window.

'Ten rupees.'

I was going to point out that the man in front of me had just paid five rupees, but then I looked at the angry scar and something inside me took control, telling me to keep quiet.

I handed him the ten, while keeping my eyes downcast.

'Get in line at the gate,' he barked. Evidently no one had told him that the customer was king.

I got in the queue. The man inside the box office now came to the gate, opened the sliding door and visually scanned the faces of those entering. Perhaps to check that only paying customers were being allowed entry.

As I entered I was assailed by a horrible smell, the origin of which I dared not guess simply because I knew what it was. To the right I saw a trickle of water running out through the gap in a closed door. On top of the door it said 'Mans'. I made a promise to myself that I would rather soil my pants than go there in case of an emergency. I also did not ask myself why there was no 'Womans'. The only 'womans' here was in everyone's minds, I remarked to myself wryly.

The hall was quite large, which was odd considering there were like thirty people. Seeing this was free seating, I took my position at an arbitrary seat. Most of the people, who I realized were regulars, gravitated to a certain section of the hall even though there was space all around. Why I understood presently.

The ancient fans, the only source of air and ventilation, were only turned on near those seats. Considering it was 40 degrees outside and not much less inside, this was most inconvenient. Yet I preferred remaining seated in the 'Devil's Crotch' – so hot and smelly that place was I can think of no other phrase to describe it – instead of sitting close to the other consumers.

City Lights started soon after as the lights inside the hall went down. About ten minutes into the movie, the black-and-white was replaced by grainy colour – a scene of writhing white bodies where the actors seemed to have no idea that they belonged to the 'silent era' so much of their pleasure they were vocalizing.

The 'punching' had begun, that esoteric art of remixing a classic like *City Lights* to make it more relevant to the audience of today.

Presently, the tramp came back. So did the blind girl. And then again, the blind girl was replaced by a naked trampy one. In colour. This alternation of characters continued throughout the length of the movie.

At one point after a particular scene, one of the audience members stood up and shouted at the projectionist:

'Play it again.'

Now for some reason that reminded me of the mythical immortal lines from *Casablanca* ['Play it again Sam'] and I wondered whether Rick had ever seen a 'gin joint' like this one.

The projector-man had his ears to the audience. I would have too if the audience was armed with daggers and country firearms. The reel was put back on and the scene was repeated much to the contented murmur of approval of the crowd. Why they were contented, again I did not need to guess. I knew.

I would have been contented too if I were not frying in the heat, scratching my posterior every ten seconds to ward off the bugs biting me, all the time mortally afraid of being beaten up by the 'regulars' for no other reason other than for not being a 'regular'.

I left the theatre just before the end credits. Perhaps I missed another 'punch'. Not that I cared.

Because by that time, whether it was from the discontinuous narrative or from the stench, I had developed quite a headache. Though I was quite sure I had seen something pretty unique – an user-interactive cinematic experience where audience members have the power to decide on the story, where no two 'shows' of the same movie are ever the same.

That was, however, not the only thing I brought back from the experience.

Two days later, I realized my bed had been infested by bedbugs.

CHAPTER 5

A Sociocultural Study of Sexual Frustration in India – More Back to the Future

Thanks for joining us after the break.

Now let us proceed to the next decade – the '90s. This was a time of great unrest, one which witnessed radical changes in the cultural, political and social life of India. Though these changes are out of the scope of the current lecture, suffice it to say that the economic liberalization that was initiated by the central government opened the gates for the invasion of satellite television, 24-hour music and movie channels. For the first time, the Indian consumer was given a choice. Did he want to see Mariah Carey in a low-cut push-up bra on channel 5 or the Union Minister for Mines opening a bauxite mining facility on state-run Channel 1? Did he want to spend his hour watching a Top 10 countdown show of sizzling music videos or did he think his time would be better spent watching a botany professor, with vegetation growing out of his ears, explain photosynthesis?

Faced with competition, the behemoth DD struck back by trying to best the cable channels at their own game with the launch of DD Metro, the name reflecting the metropolitan nature of the programmes. Of course, by virtue of being run by the same bureaucrats who ran DD in the '80s, DD Metro was severely restricted in what it could run in terms of 'popular fare'.

Very little documentary evidence of this exists but some historians claim that DD would show some English movies, late at night, which would have themes that were slightly more risqué than would have been allowed in the past. When I say a 'little more risqué' I mean that if in the '80s DD would draw the line at showing *Born Free* and *Hatari* now they would perhaps show movies that had a PG-13 rating, like *Frankenstein 90*. But even there, they would exercise snips of the scissors to remove the truly objectionable few seconds, should they exist.

This led to what are known as 'cinematic quantum effects' where the sound would not be synchronized with the visuals or when the pixelation of female flesh would be found to provide inadequate coverage. For instance, a chronicler of the '90s reported hearing a soft feminine whisper in the background while what he saw on the TV screen was a car moving over a road, the exact same scene he had seen five minutes before. A few other historians report seeing random body parts sporadically pop out from the smudged area (technically known as modesty zones) of big pixels. It goes without saying that movies like this did nothing to alleviate the sense of KLPD-ness of the general public.

As a result of this, the hungry population had no other option than to look towards foreign channels for some relief.

One of the primary avenues for titillation during prime time were the music videos that were being beamed into living rooms by MTV and Channel V, referred to in colloquial street slang as 'phoren maal'. Faced with a threat for eyeballs from beyond its shore, the Indian local movie industry struck back, taking advantage of the somewhat relaxed censorship standards (just slightly in comparison to the '80s) to pump in double-entendre-filled songs and more risqué song picturizations.

The most iconic of these songs was 'Choli ke peeche kya hai?'[English translation: 'What is behind the blouse (choli)'?] from *Khalnayak*, the textbook example of the 'bait and switch' technique that I had talked of before. Now, you there, Andrulasian in the second row, what do you think is the answer to the question 'Choli ke peeche kya hai?'

Andrulasian [with a shy nod of the head]: Humanoid female mammalian appendages...sir?

Professor: No. And I am surprised your mind is so dirty. As the second line of the song points out: the thing that resides beneath the blouse is the 'heart' ('Choli mein dil hai mera'). This is a classic example of an insidiously clever 'switch' sprung on the listener after the 'bait' of the rather provocative and possibly misleading question.

I will not go into an aesthetic analysis of this song as that is covered under the '20th Century Cultural Aesthetics', a course I teach in the Fall semester and one that I encourage you to join. In that course, along with 'Choli ke peeche kya hai' I deconstruct some of the enduring cultural artifacts of the twentieth century like 'Dhagala lagli kala' and 'Oye oye', hieroglyphic art like the famous 'If you can piss above this line, you should join the fire brigade' recovered from archaeological digs of public urinals and of course multi-volume classics like *Human Digest* and *Kamini Ki Gupt Katha*.

What I can tell you in this course, however, is that such was the effect of this song on the popular conscience that the phrase 'choli ke peeche' came to be used as a metaphor for the 'hidden truth'.

Let me illustrate with a usage example. 'Bhainsa Ram joined Crooked Party today saying he had a sudden change of heart. Now it remains to be seen choli ke peeche kya hai.'

Amdroid: You mean people were curious about what lay behind Bhainsa Ram's upper appendage covering?

Professor [ignoring the question from the literal-minded Amdroid]: Needless to say, there were ceaseless knock-offs of the 'choli ke peeche kya hai' line. First there was this innocent girl in *Dilbar* ruing the advent of her youth with the plaintive 'Main atthra baras ki ho gayee, main kya karoon, meri choli chhoti ho gayee, main kya karoon' [I have become eighteen, what to do? My blouse is splitting at the seams, what to do?]. Then there was the rambunctious Holi song (movie name: *Khalnayika*) that took the metaphorical questioning to another level with poetic lyrics that went thus:

Male: Aanchal ke andar kya hai? (What's inside the Aanchal? – the aanchal being that part of the sari used to cover the torso.)

Female: Aanchal ke andar choli. (Inside the aanchal is the blouse.)

Male: Choli ke andar kya hain? (What's inside the blouse?)

Female: Bataoon bataoon bataoon? (Shall I tell, tell, tell?)... Tabahee hai tabahee (Inside the choli is total destruction.)

The bait-and-switch paradigm is illustrated in another famous song of the '90s, that has for ages been used as an anthem for ornithologists (studiers of birds) as well as for hornithologists (horny people). The song that I am referring to is 'Gutur gutur' from the epic movie *Dalal* (Pimp). The song starts with the bait – 'Char gaya upar re' or 'It has mounted'. Then is the switch: 'Atariya pe lotan kabootar re' ('The pigeon has mounted the roof'). If you do not get the message, the director also shows scantily clad women playing around with pigeons.

As a non-graded assignment I give you these two songs and by next week, I want you to identify the bait and the switch part. The songs are provided as part of your supplementary material – they are 'Daloonga daloonga daloonga daloonga, naulakha haar tere gale mein daloonga', and 'Din mein leti hai, raat mein leti hai, subah ko leti hai, shaam ko leti hain, kya bura hai uska naam leti hain'...

Amdroid: Sir, could you please explain this with another example? My linear logic is finding this most difficult.

Professor: Uff-oh. Okay. So here is this song from a movie called *Andaaz*. The lyrics go somewhat like this: 'Khada hai khada hai, dwaar pe tere aashiq khada hai, khol khol darwaza khol, bol bol do meethe bol.' Now...

Amdroid: Yes sir. I think I got this. From my knowledge of human physiology, I can see that 'khada hai khada hai' – which can be translated to 'it is erect, it is erect' – is the bait and 'lover is standing erect at the gate' is the switch.

Enthusiastic humanoid [raising hand and hoping to curry favour with professor]: Also sir the 'khol khol khol darwaza khol' i.e. 'open the door, open the door' as it is addressed to a female may mean something else.

Professor: Well caught, humanoid. You get extra credits for that.

Humanoid male: Thank you, sir. It's just that my granddad

used to lull me to sleep with a song he said had been handed down to him by his granddad and thus through generations. It's lyrics are, 'Bholi bhali ladki khol teri dil ki pyarwali khidki ho ho ho' and from then I knew the rhetorical implications of the 'opening door'.

Professor: Your granddad is most wise. Yes, that song, an exhortation to innocent girls to open their corridor of love, was something I had left out in the discussion deliberately as I had given it as an exercise problem. No harm done. Since another song, 'Bharo maang meri bharo' from the same movie *Sabse Bada Khiladi* is already in the problem set.

Entire Class: What… problem set? Come on sir… please don't ruin our spring break.

Professor: Yes yes! I have a whole problem set where I provide the videos and accompanying translated lyrics of some songs of the '90s like 'Sarkailo khatiya', 'Kal raat saiyaan ne aisi bowling ki', 'Tururu tururu kahaan se karoon main pyar shuru' and 'Baag mein nazook nazook dal pe narangi latke'. And you will have to provide a full cultural deconstruction of the lyrics. I told you when the course began that this is not going to be an easy A.

Entire Class: Collective groan. (Or do they moan?)

As I alluded to before, the opening of the airwaves led to insidious influences not just from the west but also from the south of the country where for reasons cultural – historians have not provided a conclusive answer for – censorship standards were much slacker. There were a number of popular south Indian channels that, after the lights went out, started telecasting songs that had much more skin than was government approved. And following their antennae, teenagers all over the country would sneak out into the living room at night, with the volume turned to zero (so as not to wake up their parents in the next room), and watch entranced as buxom women – mountains of fleshy goodness often with fabric-like names, such as Silk Smitha and Nylon Nalini – shook their enormities. Thus the old adage would once again be proven – true music can be appreciated even without the sound.

Of course, that was not the only thing that was keeping young men awake at night. There were the 'After Dark Movies' like *Lake Consequence* and other works of the legendary director Zalman King. And then there was India's worst-kept secret. The fact that a Russian channel called TB6, on Saturday, and at arbitrary times late into the night would show Playboy TV, giving KLPD-ed people a glimpse of the real 'export quality' thing.

Here also we take reference to the diaries of Poltu in order to better understand the poorly understood but nevertheless fascinating cultural phenomenon known as the 'TB6 night'.

Usually we have dinner at 10:00 and Dad and Ma are asleep by 11:00. Tonight, the very night that I need them to go to bed and be sound asleep, just has to be the night that dinner is delayed. Of course I cannot tell them 'Dad, it's TB6 night. Please go to sleep and close the door for I am going to be watching naked women soap each other.' So I tell them the next thing that is closest to the truth.

'I will be doing an all-nighter. Have an assignment due on Monday.'

However, that merely explains why I need to stay awake. Not why they need to go to sleep.

Clock turns 11:00. Still no dinner. Impatient, I ask Ma, 'No dinner yet?' What I had forgotten is that the maid who cooks had vanished two days ago. Not only that, she was working for our neighbour Chowdhury aunty and Ma had been in a state of nervous breakdown ever since. She snaps back at me saying she is not bonded labour and that I should be grateful for the services I take as my birthright. Presently, Dad too gets involved and I am assailed by two air-raid sirens that drone on and on.

Now usually I don't much care about being shouted at but today I really need this to stop. So I quickly apologize. Dinner is eaten soundlessly. The good thing is that by 12:00, dinner is over. I do not mention that there was double the salt in the egg curry. Mercifully, even Dad stays silent.

The thing about Playboy TV on TB6 is that the time of telecast is never fixed. The hour could be as early as 12 (in which case I was out of luck tonight) or as late as 4. Praying that tonight was not a 12 night, I even help my mother with the dishes so that she gets finished quickly. Mom thinks that I am being contrite for the incident earlier. This puts her in a comparatively better mood.

Good.

And just when I think that I am going to get exclusive access to the living room, Dad suddenly decides this is the night he is going to watch some post-supper TV. Ma joins him.

Needless to say, this is disaster. I keep pacing up and down from the study into the living room, each time expecting to hear a tired, 'It's late, let's go to bed.' No such luck. 1:15 becomes 1:30. I start coming in so often and with such an irritated expression on my face that Dad, who is somewhat perceptive asks, 'Is there any problem? Do you want to watch something?'

Too close to the truth, I say, 'No no, not at all. I have a submission,' and go back to my study with my ears open, listening for the shuffling of my dad's feet or for the TV being turned off. At around 2:30, I think I see Dad's back. At 2:35 the bedroom lights go off.

Good.

I tiptoe, keeping the lights off. I turn the TV on. The bluish glow washes the room and I look nervously towards my parent's bedroom (they never sleep with their doors closed), hoping they are too fast asleep to notice the light. Flipping the channel to TB6, I find there is some programme on.

Since everyone has their clothes on it is of absolutely no interest to me.

I am now in a quandary. Have I missed tonight's entertainment? Or is it still to come? I obviously cannot go to bed without confirming that. But how long can I...

Rustle rustle, I hear. Damn! Someone has woken up. I quickly turn the TV off and the bluish glow flickers out just in time. Dad comes in. He sees that I am sitting in a dark room, face towards the TV with the TV off. He stands in the corridor silently looking at me, expecting an answer.

I mumble something on the lines of, 'Was just taking a break. Getting some air.'

It is a good excuse. Except for two small reasons.

First of all I am 'getting air' sitting in a room where all windows are closed, even though my study has an attached balcony.

Second, the red light is still blinking on the panel of the TV, signifying that it had just been on.

Dad looks sternly at me and says, 'If your work is finished, go to sleep.'

Of course my work might very well have finished. Or it might not even have started. I wait till Dad goes to sleep. Or pretends to.

I come back at around 3 a.m. No nothing. I immediately switch off the TV and hurry back. Good thing I do because in a minute, Dad comes back to go to the bathroom. Or perhaps just to catch me red-handed. But this time, all he sees is an empty living room and my study light on. He goes back.

Against my better judgement, I go back. Again and again like an aircraft on strafing runs. But no, my luck is out. Then around 5, just as I am going to call it a night, I turn it on and staring back at me is the greatest expanse of female flesh that has ever graced my humble TV.

Yessss!!!! And I can even hear Dad and Ma snoring in tandem.

Nestling securely onto the couch, I am starting to relax when...

The flesh tones shrivel to a dot.

The power has gone.

Load shedding, that curse of Kolkata.

Trying to get up and rush out, my knee bangs onto the coffee table, sending the books tumbling down. Woken up by the sound of the falling books and by the fact that the ceiling fan has stopped, my dad cries out:

'Are you still in the living room?'

Damn.

But this state of late night bliss could not go on for long without a blowback of epic proportions. If you recall, the rulers of India had total power over their subjects and while the nanny state's consistent apathy towards ensuring the physical and economic security of its citizens has been well-documented, they never failed in making sincere attempts to safeguard the moral health of the nation.

With people just like our Poltu all across the land, lying awake at night and reporting to school/college with their eyes bloodshot and their brains full of happy thoughts, it became obvious that fatty flesh-toned cholesterol deposits were clogging up the nation's moral arteries. In the face of this incorporeal health crisis, the government was forced to crack down with an iron fist on the cable channels that were serving up this grease of turpitude in the hope that activities that could lead to carpal tunnel syndrome at best and eternal damnation in the after-life at worst could be somewhat subdued.

Cable channels were asked to clean up their act. Those who complied stayed on. Those who did not were blocked.

With the sources of release thus choked by fiat, the citizens became increasingly desperate. By this time, however, a revolutionary technology was making its presence felt across the land.

The Internet.

True it was very expensive, Net speeds were like those of a six–month-old toddler and access limited to only the privileged few. However, once someone got hold of this precious resource, be it at work, at school or at their rich uncle's house, they just refused to let go.

And why the hell would you? 'Cause once you got on that information superhighway, that freeway of love, no information and broadcasting minister could hold you back.

In the words of Martin Luther King Junior, you were 'free free free at last, thank God almighty you were free at last'.

And what a freedom it was. Freedom from the pixellated world of DD, from the severely vegetarian fare of English movie channels, from the corpulent carcasses of the southern channels and from dingy run-down cinema theatres in the backwaters of the city.

Pleasure was now just a mouse-click away.

In this context, it is worth mentioning an interesting hypothesis that has been put forward by that great historian of information technology, Satyam Shivam. The hypothesis, called 'Quickly Minimize Windows Hypothesis', was proposed by Mr Shivam to account for the genesis of the Indian IT industry, the inexorable economic force that propelled India to the status of a world power by the 2050s.

One of the persistent historical conundrums that have befuddled experts over the ages is why India, as opposed to Japan or China, was able to take an early adopter advantage in software. This is doubly mysterious when one considers how Japan dominated the electronics and the automotive market and China was the undisputed king of cheap manufacturing, lead-filled toys and American Chop Suey, while in contrast, India's automotive, electronics and manufacturing industries lagged far far behind. So what was so special about software and programming that brought out the latent potential of a nation, otherwise so lacklustre in taking the initiative in adopting technological trends?

Were, as some proposed, Indians more mathematically inclined towards programming than the Chinese and the Japanese? Was India's domination of the IT domain due to the forward-thinking policies of the government?

Satyam Shivam proposes an interesting explanation, one which in my opinion and of other scholars sounds the most reasonable.

According to him, the high KLPD state of the Indian population combined with government/societal moral repression that sought to cut off every other avenue of release, pushed an entire generation to the Internet as a source of liberation.

Now obviously, in order to gain access to the Internet, which was then an extremely costly resource, there had to be some solid reason. One could not just go to Dad and say, 'Dad, buy me a computer, and yeah, also pony up some dough for an Internet connection so that I can watch Pamela Anderson.'

Instead one could couch the desire for Internet and computer access in a more acceptable cocoon: ' Dad, I really love computers and programming. Uncle Gupta tells me that computers are the wave of the future. Can you please put off Ma's operation for two years so that we can buy a computer?' Or, 'Dad, I really need the Internet to apply abroad, check out the websites of universities, email professors and write some web applications.'

Indian parents, being the trusting gentle species they are and not quite understanding this new-fangled thingie and the way it may be (mis)used, bought their little lambkins computers. After all, what's an advance on your provident fund when your offspring's future is at stake?

And so it came to pass that many young people suddenly had these marvellous machines in their bedrooms.

But then, even the most trusting parents do sneak behind you every now and then in order to check their return on investment.

Hence an entire generation started writing code, purely as a diversionary tactic so that their real game was never busted, so that when Mum came to say, 'Sunil beta, dinner is ready,' that 'other' screen could quickly be minimized and a blue Turbo-Pascal editor would come up with a 'Compiling Code' message written boldly, so boldly that Mum would feel proud that Sunil was doing something of great importance, important enough for her to grin and bear the pain of those pesky kidney stones.

Slowly and surely, these serial minimizers started getting proficient in their code-hacking skills, no doubt because of the long hours spent tinkering with C and Java, waiting for their parents to go to bed. Now the guys elsewhere, in other countries, under more liberal moral regimes never felt this visceral desire to get on the Net simply because their biological urges had alternative avenues (namely unfettered fraternization with the female species) for gratification. Hence programming never really caught on in these places, definitely not as rapidly and as early as it caught on in India.

However, it was not smooth sailing for the pioneers of the late '90s. First of all, for many voyagers their access to the Internet was through what was known as a shell account. This type of Internet access was much cheaper than a normal Internet (or what was known as a TCP/IP) account. The only catch with the shell account was that it allowed the user to navigate through the web using a browser called Lynx which, horror of horrors, provided no support for graphics or video.

That's right, class.

It was like being blindfolded with the knowledge that there were beauties standing behind a glass, while all you could do was grope in the dark, your nails scratching impotently against the surface while the world laughed at you, with a KLPD-inducing message (Inline Image) marking the spot where the heavenly visage of Cindy Crawford would have been, had you enough money for a TCP/IP account.

Even for those who got their teeth into a TCP/IP account, there were still thorns on the path of salvation. Most prickly of these was that American and European exotic websites required users to provide their credit cards for their monthly services. Even those services that claimed to be free (such sites were never really free as people soon realized when their hard drive filled up mysteriously with spyware and other malicious applications) had age verification. Credit cards those days in India, before the call centre revolution, were inaccessible for most twenty-somethings and so once again, the youth were locked out of moksha, this time for not possessing a teeny weeny bit of plastic.

But it is darkest just before dawn. And when things were the worst, the saviour came along.

And what was that?

A South-Asian-themed website maintained in one of the Taliban theocracies, then jointly called Pakistan, which went by the name of Desibaba. Inspired by the spirit of free, open-source software ('software, like sex, is best when free'), Desibaba dispensed with the need of payments and credit cards, instead choosing to rely on a fully advertiser-driven revenue model. Intrinsically trusting of its audience when they said they were over the age of eighteen, Desibaba did not bother itself with formalities like age verification but instead concentrated on customer service by giving people what they came for – flesh-coloured pixels. Like the best of premier restaurants, it served eclectic fare: a full-fledged Indian menu but with enough cross-cultural cuisine to keep even the most internationally minded foodie happily munching late into the night.

Humanoid: Are these specimens included in the supplementary lecture notes?

Professor: Emm no. But if you pay me ten Universal Currency, I can get them for you after class.

In any case, Desibaba was not just about stimulating the visual cortex. It also had enough textual material about Bengali boudis (sisters-in-law) and Chennai aunties written in an English style that cunning linguists have called 'unfettered, free-form without regard to conventional rules of grammar' to keep even the most demanding bibliophile happy. In an age where digital image processing was still in its infancy, Desibaba pioneered the arcane craft of morphing, the art of taking pictures of famous actresses and superimposing their faces onto the body of ordinary women. Added to such technological marvels were the added bonuses of regular updates, no dead links and just five pop-ups for every page loaded, and one begins to understand how Desibaba became such a national underground rage, spawning spin-offs and cheap imitations like Desimama and Chalugirl.

Android: So what happened to this marvellous source of joy and information?

Professor: Very interesting question. We shall discuss this in the next class. But in a few years, the dot-com revolution of the late '90s ran out of steam and the pure advertiser-driven revenue model became discredited. The Indian adult market caught the attention of multinational exotic businesses and stiff competition was mounted, mostly dishonestly, by passing off Hispanic/Mexican women as asli desi ghee latikas. Credit cards became more accessible with the outsourcing era and yuppies had more choice. Censor boards became more liberal. The age of 'Item Girls' and 'Serial Kissers' was going to start, giving a new meaning and direction to the cultural and intellectual development of a nation.

For today's lecture, I will conclude by reading a diary extract from the legendary Poltu in which we are told of what happened when one of his college mates got a TCP/IP connection and invited a group of friends to his house.

It was Tuesday that Neel told us that the TCP/IP connection, the one that gives you full access to dirty pictures... sorry graphics... has finally arrived at his place. Thank goodness that at least one of our dads had the good sense and the bank balance to understand that the blackened-out view of the Internet our shell accounts gave us was severely compromising our learning experience. Now if only my father would realize the fact.

Ah well.

After college, four of us friends (all guys of course) are scheduled to go to Neel's place and get some Internet study done. As I ride footboard on the crowded mini-bus with my nose nestled in the smelly armpit of a middle-aged man sweating a river, I keep telling myself that this torture, inhuman as it is, is still worth it.

For the sake of education.

After all, great men of generations past would sit below street lights to study, for years on end. Compared to that what was the discomfort of an hour of enduring the fragrance of a steamy, sweaty rainforest?

Absolutely insignificant.

On arrival, we enter Neel's bedroom where the portal to a world of edutainment is going to go 'khul jaa sim sim' in a few minutes. Neel seems to be strangely jumpy and almost stand-offish as if he was already regretting letting slip the news of this wonderful addition to his family.

'Only fifteen minutes. The company has given only 100 hours Net-time to my dad. And the telephone charges we have to pay out of our own pocket. So that's it. Fifteen minutes time on the dial-up.'

Prateek, who had brought a whole case of floppy discs to back up the pictures that we would download, is dismayed.

'What! You got to be kidding me. Fifteen minutes! With the pathetic Net-speed, we would be fortunate to get ten pictures in that time. Look here, do you want the Cindy Crawford collection I got from my cousin in the US or not?'

Neel is in the midst of a moral quandary.

'Okay… twenty minutes… not a minute more.'

Rajesh, the scaredy cat among us, speaks.

'Neel. What about the door? We should close it. Looking at how your PC faces the door, Aunty can walk in any moment and get a full view of the screen.'

Neel squeaks.

'Yeah right, genius. Close that and make it obvious to Ma that we are doing something that we should not. Shutting the door is just inviting trouble.'

'It's okay,' I say. 'You guys stand here around the screen, pretending to watch some demo of interest. Let me drive this one. I am going to copy as many pictures as we can in the half an hour...'

'Twenty, I said twenty.'

'...in the twenty minutes we have online, and then we can copy the pictures onto the floppies, take them home, and watch them at leisure after-hours. And Sando, you keep a ear open for any footsteps nearby. If you hear something, just shout, "Assignment done."

'Got it. I will shout "Assignment Done" at the first sign of trouble,' Sando assures us.

I really like Sando. He is a reliable guy.

So we take our formations. I am on the chair with the mouse in hand. Neel is biting his nails just behind me. Flanking me on either side are Rajesh and Prateek. Sando is on the lookout behind.

The sound of the modem dialing the line is followed by that of the connection being made. My heart is beating fast.

'Password?' I ask.

Neel comes to the keyboard and types it in. Of course, for some reason we can scarcely fathom, he does not trust us with the password.

I look up at Prateek.

That is because both Prateek and I had noted the password Neel typed in, considering how slow his fingers move.

It is, very predictably, 'sharonstone69'.

We exchange knowing smiles.

And then, in front of us, in full colour it comes up, like a magical genie from the phone-lines.

The Internet.

And it beckons like a heroine in a see-through chiffon sari, winking and biting her lip.

At that moment, I think I understand exactly how Moses must have felt as he stood on the hill and gazed at the Promised Land.

My reverie is disturbed by Neel muttering 'Twenty minutes twenty minutes' in a state of nervous excitement.

I had done some prep work regarding exactly where we want to go. So no time is wasted in searching. We get right to the chase.

A full page of thumbnail pictures come up, albeit slowly.

Neel mutters, 'Faster faster guys.'

I snap at him. 'Look here, Neel. This is your connection which is taking time. So stop snapping at me.'

The page loads.

I ask the guys, 'Okay, tell me which of these should we load full-size?'

Soon everyone is talking, pointing to different places on the screen.

'This one.'

'No this one'

'This first.'

'Are you crazy? No way we waste time on that one. Neel has bigger ones than that girl.'

Neel scowls. He is a competitive person.

'Of course I do.'

Prateek, Rajesh and I stifle our laughs. No time to be wasted on ribbing Neel about this faux-pas. The rest of his life waits.

I move as quickly as possible. As a full-sized picture finishes loading, I right-click and do a 'Save As'.

Soon I have gotten into a steady rhythm of 'Save As'. The Net connection is rather good. The pictures are loading decently quickly. The only pause occurs when a spectacular image opens up in its full glory, distracting me from the task at hand. Yes, God does exist. He sure does.

I feel heavy breathing on the back of my neck. Everyone has gone quiet.

Someone says in hushed tones, 'So that's how it looks like.'

We lose our sense of time.

Suddenly the magic of the moment is broken by a cheerful female voice: 'Here is some tea and cakes for you hardworking boys'.

Oh God! It is Neel's mother. In the room.

How the hell did this happen? Was Sando not the watch-out man?

Evidently not. Instead of keeping watch at the door, Sando had moved forward and like all of us, had his eyes glued to the screen. No wonder he never heard the footsteps nor did he realize that Aunty had wandered into the room.

Sando is a reliable guy. Did I just say that a few paragraphs ago? I take it back.

There is panic. But she still has not seen the screen. A gurgling sound comes from Neel.

Plan B. With my finger flying, my mouse cursor goes to the minimize button and I click on it.

The browser window shrinks to a bar at the bottom.

At the sudden movement, Aunty's eyes are drawn to the screen.

No problem. Because all she will get to see is a nice background wallpaper of green leaves.

Relief!

But nooooo! As the window minimizes and the background is revealed, there are no green leaves.

Instead there is a picture of two well-equipped clothing-deficient women kissing each other.

I freeze. A sick feeling rises up from the pit of my stomach and reaches for my chest. A pang of horror.

In a flash, I realize what I have done.

In the excitement of discovery, while right-clicking and scrolling down to the 'Save As' option, I had missed my click.

And I had selected, by mistake, the 'Set as Desktop Background' option.

In the reflection on screen, I catch Aunty's shocked face as an audible 'Lord save us' escapes her lips and the tray with the tea cups starts shaking…

Neel is the first one to speak.

'I have no idea how that…'

All of us have frozen in panic.

Rajesh reacts first. He yanks out the power chord hoping to turn the blasted machine off immediately.

Nothing happens.

Prateek, sounding like a headless chicken says, 'Neel! You have a UPS backup power supply...?'

By this time, I realize we are far beyond pretending. I do what I should have done a few seconds back.

I switch off the screen.

Aunty keeps the tea and cake on the table wordlessly. The smile has vanished. Neel is sitting on the bed, his head in his hands. Prateek is looking at me with daggers in his eyes.

And then, breaking the 'itna sannata jo hai' cloud, Sando says, a lifetime too late:

'Ass...ass...assignment done.'

I don't think I will ever go back to Neel's house again.

Chapter 6

A Short Story on Terror

Scene 1

Kasai sits on the steamer as it moves down the muddy waters towards an Indian city (let's call it K). He looks suspiciously at his fellow passengers all of whom are playing bridge and talking to themselves loudly.

He, however, is silent. He is nervous. The sweat rolls down his brow.

Somewhere up above a crow defecates on his shoulder.

He barely notices.

He curses his luck. If only he had not detonated the bomb two minutes too early and almost killed the ISI colonel who was teaching them urban warfare in the LET camp, he would not have come last in class. And what a horrible punishment had that been. Just for one instant of performance anxiety. While the first three had secured bumper Jihadi contracts and a promise of the choicest of virgins in heaven, here he was alone heading towards K. The lone citizen from the 'Land of the Poor'. His crew consists of Bangladeshis. He has little faith in them. They have not been trained. And worse, their Urdu is horrible, they speak to each other in Bengali, several have pot bellies and he doubts how much he can depend on them when the shit hits the fan.

But he will have to make do. It is his operation. He has to make it work.

SCENE 2

It's morning. They make ground. Kasai and his crew of five grab their equipment. Kasai tells his Bangladeshis: 'You know the plan. We shoot random people on the streets. Then we go into the Super Luxury Hotel, shoot people in the restaurants, kill the staff and hold the foreign guests hostage.' One of the Bangladeshis, chewing a pan, says something like, 'E hala to dekhi sudhu bakphottai maira zaaye,' to which the others laugh. Kasai chooses to ignore, simply because he has no clue as to what the man had just said. [What they said was: 'This saala just keeps talking the talk.']

SCENE 3

The group reaches their first action point. But wait, something is wrong. Kasai knits his brow. There are no people in the streets. Who the hell is he supposed to shoot at? There are two charred public buses on the road. He feels afraid. Has he goofed up again? Did some other group of terrorists already come and do their job? Had he come too late? But no. That cannot be.

Presently he catches sight of a man walking on the street. He reaches inside his backpack to pull his AK47 out but then realizes he needs to know what is going on. He walks upto the man and says, 'Eh you, why is there no one on the road?'

The man sneers, 'What kind of a man are you? Don't you read the papers. There is a general strike going on. No one dares to comes out on road, sir. See what her supporters did to these buses. This is, wait, let me see, the twentieth such bandh we have had this year. I am a daily labourer. These bandhs will kill us all. I tell you. By the way you want to get your shoulder cleaned. A crow has shat on it.'

Kasai feels his stomach knotting up. No people on the streets! Oh man. This operation hasn't even begun and already the first part has failed. No problem.

He thinks of shooting the man. But no, killing the first person you see is bad luck. He does not need more of it.

He turns to his crew, 'On to the hotel.'

SCENE 4

Kasai and his group barge into the hotel with Kasai holding his AK47 in front of him. He sees a large lobby. To his right and left are two places which look like they could be restaurants. He bursts into one ready to shoot. Empty. He rushes to the other. That's empty too. The lobby is empty. He shoots one shot into the air. And shouts: 'Come out, you dogs. Death is here.'

A spectacled man in his sixties, thin and emaciated, in a white dhoti, comes out and stands behind the desk in the lobby. He says in a calm voice, 'No need to shout. I am coming. Oh, at last. You guys are from pest control, right? You are like one year late.'

Kasai waves the AK47 at him and says, 'We are not from pest control, you dog. We are here to take revenge for Gujarat,

Kashmir, Palestine and for not making Zaheer the winner of reality music show *Gaata Chal*. Now where are the people in the restaurants?'

The man behind the lobby doesn't lose his cool. Adjusting his ancient glasses, one of which is held to his ear by a string, he says, 'Oh my. Terrorists. My friends, who sent you here?'

Kasai screams, 'Not your problem, old man. I asked you a question.'

The man says, 'If you have not noticed, there is a bandh going on. Plus, even at the best of times no one comes to these restaurants. If you have ever tried the food here, you would have known why. Ever since the government took over the operations, things have been like…'

Kasai once again feels a cold sweat running down his back. Trying to control himself he says, 'Okay. Stand still. We will kill the guests. Aieeee, everyone go upstairs and start shooting.'

The man says, 'Hold it, hold it. First of all, the contractors who repaired this hotel three years ago put sand instead of cement and stole all the genuine stuff. So if you guys go on shooting arbitrarily, it's you who will be dead before long as the ceiling and the walls will fall on you. Second of all, there are no guests in this hotel.'

Kasai says, 'W-ha-tttt? A five-storey hotel without guests? You mean to say there are no foreigners.'

The man says, 'Yes sir. That is exactly what I am saying. Why would anyone want to come here? There is nothing here any longer. Foreigners? Hah! Dear sir, we have made sure that there are no investments in this state by capitalists. We have made this city into a foreigner and capitalist free zone. No Westerner comes here. Neither do businessmen from any corner of the world.'

A sound comes from upstairs. The unmistakable sound of footsteps.

Kasai smiles. 'Very brave old man. Protecting your guests with that lie? You will now die.'

The old man shakes his head. 'Not very bright, are you? Those footsteps you heard upstairs are of mice. Gigantic mice. They run all over the place. I thought you guys were here because of them...'

Kasai barks, 'We will check that. So where are the cooks, waiters, the hotel employees? Bring them out now.'

The man shakes his head mournfully. 'That was what I was trying to tell you, sir. Ever since the government took over the operations, there has been a strike as none of the five employee unions have been able to come to an agreement. Here you can fire a person by shooting him with a gun but you cannot fire him by taking away his job. Even when he does nothing. The short of it is there have been no employees here for many years. Those red flags you see of various shades all around aren't works of art. They are union flags.'

Kasai's voice breaks. 'Then why are you here?'

The man says, 'Long story. I stay here out of habit. I worked for fifty years. Grew up in this place. Now I no longer get paid. But I just stay here out of hope that maybe some day... Plus I don't have a house...'

Kasai now feels very sick. 'Shut up, you dog. No one wants to hear your life-story. Oh my, what am I going to do now!'

SCENE 5

Half an hour later. Kasai stands again in front of the old man.

'Seems you were right. There are no people in this blasted place. Wait. This is state government property. I can hold the building hostage.'

The old man says, 'Oh dear lord. Government property means it's no one's property. No one cares. People don't give a rat's ass here if old manuscripts are stolen or if heritage buildings get destroyed by promoters.'

Kasai says, 'We will see about that. Plus the government cannot be sure there are no people here. Once the cops and commandos come, we will have real people to shoot at. Okay let's see, here is a phone book... Mmmm... Police station... Okay old man call this number. And tell them that terrorists have entered the hotel and taken people hostage.'

'I am sorry sir. The phone has been out of order. No one paid the phone repair man their baksheesh. So...'

Kasai snarls, 'What a hellhole this is.'

He brings out his satellite phone and starts dialling the number.

The phone at the other end keeps ringing.

Presently someone picks it up.

An immensely disinterested voice says, 'Hello.'

Kasai says, 'Listen carefully. I am a jihadi terrorist and along with my jihadi brothers we have taken foreigners hostage at the Super Luxury Hotel and will start killing them, one every fifteen minutes. We have already killed... emmm... many.'

The voice at other end: 'Super Luxury Hotel, you say?'

Kasai says, 'Yes yes.'

The voice says: 'Not our jurisdiction. Call Park Place thana.'

Kasai says, 'Listen you. Did you just hear what I said? I am going to...'

The voice becomes irritated. 'Yes I heard what you said. Did you hear what I said? I will watch you on television just like everyone else. Kahan kahan se chale aate hain…'

Phone disconnects.

Kasai is seething with rage. This he did not bargain for.

Kasai looks at the old man.

'He hung up on me. Saying it's not his jurisdiction. Whattttt……… Okay, let me get Park Place…'

He dials again.

It is presently picked up.

Kasai says, 'I am a jihadi terrorist. And along with my jihadi brothers we have taken foreigners hostage at the Super Luxury Hotel and will start killing them, one every fifteen minutes.'

The voice says, 'So what should I do?'

Kasai is stunned.

'Come here, of course.'

The voice replies, 'This is a strike day. You expect us to go? You come here to the thana and file an FIR.'

Kasai replies, 'I am a jihadi terrorist and you expect me to come and file a FIR at the thana?'

'Look jihadi, azadi, barbadi, whatever you are. If you want the police to come, you come here and file a FIR. Understand? These laatsahabs expect us to drive down on a strike day. Scoot.'

Phone disconnects.

SCENE 6

Kasai sits on the stairs. Thinking. What is he going to do now? He is about to put a call to Pakistan when his eyes alight on his Bangladeshi crew. They are unpacking.

'What the hell is that? I thought you guys were supposed to bring RDX.'

One of the Bangladeshi men say, 'Look here. We are not your slaves. You were supposed to bring it. We brought coal stoves and a large cache of hilsa fish. You told us to be prepared for a long siege and so we brought a lot of food. And spices. And coal. Kalu Miyan here can make a spicy fish curry.'

Kasai does not know whether to laugh or cry.

'Hilsa fish? Stove? You guys were supposed to bring dry fruits and get as much explosives as you could...'

The Bangladeshi man loses his temper. 'Kasai Khan, you may be a Pathan, we are not. We don't eat dry fruits. Look here, since you are not using your satellite phone, can I use it to call my Khatun Bibi?'

Kasai hisses.

'If I don't get anyone to kill by the next hour, as God is my witness, I will start killing you guys off...'

SCENE 7

Presently, there is a commotion. Kasai's face lights up. There are people at the gates.

'Quick all of you lock and load.'

The door of the hotel opens. Kasai takes his position.

A politician stands with an angry expression on his face. Behind him are a gang of people, many with long kurtas and pyjamas.

The old man behind the counter whispers, 'Oh my God. They are here.'

SCENE 8

The politician takes no notice of the AK47 pointed at him. He walks up to Kasai.

'I just heard that someone checked into the Super Luxury Hotel. Look here, you punk. I don't know what exploitative capitalist enterprise you want to set up here but I am sure it's not good for farmers, street hawkers and auto-drivers. We don't like your kind here. So just leave before I do to you what I have done to anyone who has ever dared to open shop or do any kind of progress in this state.'

Kasai says: 'Relax. I am not here to start any business. I am here to do jihad. Yes. Terrorize. Burn. Make people afraid. Stop all life.'

The politician turns to the people and gestures in an exasperated way.

'This keeps getting better and better. So you are here to terrorize people. Hmm. Make them afraid. Stop all life. Now listen carefully, you piece of shit. THAT IS MY SOLE EXCLUSIVE AREA OF BUSINESS. I HAVE THE MONOPOLY. Do you understand? How dare you try to muscle in on my turf? I will make life so much hell for you, boy, you will regret the day you ever decided to come to my city. I have brought to knees bigger fish. You are just a punk.'

SCENE 9

A soft voice comes along and steps between Kasai and the politician who are eyeballing each other viciously.

'Please, please, let us not get agitated here.'

Kasai waves his AK47 threateningly.

'Who the hell are you?'

The bearded man says, 'I am just a humble intellectual. These are all my intellectual friends. We all came here thinking you were an industrialist and a capitalist and needed to be protested against but now we realize you are also an exploited. Come, let us all hold hands.'

Kasai yells, 'Stay away. Keep your distance.'

The bearded man says: 'I compose tuneless songs, sing them badly and think highly of myself. Sometimes I do not even know what I am protesting against but as long as I can get some attention I do it nonetheless. This here is a famous poet. Famous dissident. Against industrialization... That there is another famous singer who is also a famous dissident. Against, you guessed it, industrialization!'

Kasai feels surrounded. He strengthens his grip on the trigger. There is something threatening about these slightly effete people with beards, something he cannot put a finger on.

The bearded man says, 'Don't worry Jihadi-bhai. We are all here to see if we can get together for something...'

Scene 10

It is then that Kasai has a revelation. Whether it is because of the intellectuals checking him out greedily, or whether it is the politician glaring ferociously that trigerred it, Kasai knows not. But at last he understands.

The fundamental truth.

Politicians and so-called intellectuals are the true agents of terror. Not him. As long as they stay here, this place will always be a graveyard. A terrorist can only inflict a few days of damage. These people can do the same thing but spread it over generations. Killing them would put a body count against

Kasai's name. True. Maybe he will even get half a virgin in heaven.

But the larger jihadi mission of spreading terror and stifling development in this part of the country would fail.

As a great man once said, 'You need to lose in order to win.'

And sometimes you need to give life in order to kill.

Kasai says,'Okay. I surrender. Just let me walk out of here with my crew.'

One Bangladeshi says: 'You leave if you want to. We are not leaving. Politician-uncle, please give us fake ration cards. We will become part of your party. None of us came here with bad intentions. We just want to settle down in India.'

The politician smiles benignly.

'That can be arranged. But you have to pass the three tests before I give you your ration cards. You have to successfully block a road for twelve hours, burn one item of public property and play a part in stalling at least one development project. As for you, Pakistani, I give you three hours to leave the city.'

SCENE 11:

Kasai stands outside.

Smoke is bellowing from one of the windows of Super Luxury Hotel. But not in the way Kasai thought it would. Kalu Miyan and his friends are cooking up a storm using their coal stove. The smell of fish permeates the air. The intellectuals are milling about, hoping to have yet another free dinner.

Once again Kasai is alone. Peeling the crow shit off the shoulder of his shirt, he looks heavenwards.

And for the first time in many hours, many days, and perhaps many years, he smiles.

CHAPTER 7

Politics Is the Last Refuge

Corrupt.

Incompetent.

In bed with criminals.

Loyal only to themselves and their offsprings.

Stop it. Stop it right there.

As Shatrughan Sinha (himself an actor who became a politician, or was it the other way round?) would say: 'Khamosh‼ Ek aur lavs nikala to…'

Nothing makes me as hot under the collar as the persistently negative portrayal of Indian politicians in the popular media. Surely these patriotic men and women deserve more for lifetimes of selfless service provided in exchange for the most meagre of remuneration.

Ok, here's the deal. Can you please tell me, why are almost all politicians in Hindi movies played by character actors like Sadhashiv Amrapurkar and Om Puri? Why do we never find perfectly torsoed Hrithik Roshan or his identical copy Harman Baweja essaying the role of a minister?

Yes, I know you do not know the answer. Okay then. Try this. Why do Hindi movies have dialogues of this kind:

'Aajkal gundagiri aur netagiri ek hi baap ke do harami aulaad hain.'[1]

[English translation: In today's world, the mafia and the politician are the two bastard sons of the same father.]

Needless to say, such slinging of mud at this group of most noble and able patriots offends me. Which is why I use this chapter to demolish certain myths about Indian politicians that may have taken root in your mind, thanks to the hopelessly lopsided, misbalanced coverage they get in the popular media.

In other words, I am going to act as the PR agent for an entire profession.

Free of cost.[2]

MYTH 1: MOST INDIAN POLITICIANS ARE TOO OLD FOR THE JOB

'You are old, Father William,' the young man said,
'And your hair has become very white;
And yet you incessantly stand on your head –
Do you think, at your age, it is right?'
'In my youth,' Father William replied to his son,
'I feared it would injure the brain;

---

1 From the movie *Gunda* (1998).

2 Also because I want to be a politician myself one day. If you read this previous sentence, it means you are thoroughly going through the book – including the part no one bothers to read – the footnotes. Good for you.

But now that I'm perfectly sure I have none,
Why, I do it again and again.'[3]

Yes, it is true that Indian politicians are by and large extremely old. [The exceptions being the sons of other extremely old politicians.] But why does advanced age necessarily imply obsolescence, impaired decision-making and an overall failure to keep up with changing times?

As Sourav Ganguly used to say through the last few of years of his career, when his place was perennially under the sword, no matter how well he batted: 'What does age have to do with performance?'

Though Pfizer, which sells Viagra, might have some different ideas on the relationship between age and performance, I kind of agree with Dada.

First of all, the job of running the country and taking critical decisions that touch the lives of billions of people is exactly the kind of stuff people in their seventies and above should be doing. After all, what job is more suited to senior citizens than one that has no fixed hours, no criteria for evaluation of performance, provides rest, relaxation and travel on the money of others (taxpayers), and asks for nothing more than the dispensation of advice, speeches and grand designs? I agree that the idea of political decision-makers dozing off during discussions of national import may be a bit disquieting, but hey, which one of us has not fallen asleep at an office meeting?

The most important thing is that old politicians have a sense of history, having seen a lot of it happening in front of their eyes. That is in itself a great thing.

---

3 From *Alice in Wonderland* by Lewis Carroll.

Just to make things clear, my endorsement of old people has a lot to do with my mistrust of the younger generation. After all, a generation that has me as one of its members cannot be really considered to be reliable or sound.

Let's face it. Young people should make all of us nervous. Some of them have new ideas. (I myself don't.) Worse, some of them have idealism. Even worse, some of them may actually get things done. (A few are actually doing that – again not me.) I am not sure I want my ancient country being run by such people. At the very least, I do not think it is wise to let a person who has grown up mashing Playstation controllers while blowing up imaginary aliens being given the nuclear button.

Do you?

Much better to let old people control the wheel, even if they sometimes fall asleep there.

Myth 2: Most Indian politicians are corrupt

Nothing could be further from the truth. Sure, some of our elected and on-the-verge-of-being-elected officials have made some money. To the tune of crores of rupees. It is also not beyond the realms of impossibility that their spouses, sons and pet dogs may own cars, farmland, bungalows, millions in cash and other trifles. There may also be certain accounts in a country where Yash Chopra loves to shoot movies[4] that may have some connection with certain politicians.

---

4 That place being Switzerland where the hills are forever alive with the sounds of Lata Mangeshkar going 'La la La La La La La' and where the bankers hold Indians in high esteem.

But what's wrong with that? Just because they make a whole lot of cash, are we supposed to consider politicians 'corrupt'?

Surely not.

The underlying assumption behind the myth of political corruption is obvious – the people whose decisions and words of advice bring peace, prosperity and keep the nation 'shining' are expected not to benefit from their years of toil. So while no eyebrows are raised when corporate head-honchos take in eight-figure salaries and many times that in perks, poor politicians are dragged over the coals for accepting the most trivial of remunerations – a flat or a car or a suitcase full of cash. Things are so bad that these poor folks have to spend so much time, which could otherwise have been spent in improving the lot of the people, in hiding the fruits of their labour just so that we do not get the wrong ideas.

When you go to a restaurant, you leave something extra for the waiter. Why? You do it so as 'To Insure Prompt Service' (acronymed as TIPS). It is not as if the waiter is not being paid by the restaurant. Yet you give something extra to the waiter as a premium for service rendered.

Is that corruption?

No.

Similarly, when you take your child to a school and the principal asks for a 'donation' so as to admit the student, is that corruption?

Again the answer is, no. This financial transaction is, as the name suggests, a voluntary 'donation', a contribution you as a parent make, from the goodness of your heart, in exchange for your child's academic future. And if you cannot exhibit even this amount of generosity, then what lessons of 'charity begins at home' will you impart to the little one?

By a similar reasoning, a dowry is a payment that you, as the parent of the bride, make to the husband's family as ransom money in exchange for a guarantee that nothing untoward will happen to your daughter.

Oh, I am sorry, I did not mean that. The words came out all wrong.

So let me rephrase that.

Just as a dowry is a payment that you, as the parent of the bride, make to your own daughter so that she can start off her life happily in the husband's family.

Again, is that corruption?

We all know the answer.

Still don't get what I am driving at?

No problem.

Here is another example. Your building plans are at the corporation office. Or say you have a loan application. There is a man sitting in front of you behind a table full of files, chewing on a paan, who totally disregards your patient queries from the other end of the table and buries himself absolutely in his work – reading the daily newspaper. At this point of time, what do you do?

I think I know.

Out of your own volition, you take out a bundle of Rs 100 notes from your pocket, which you then gently slip to the officious attendant standing nearby so that sahib can have a pack of Gold Flakes (or Dunhills, depending on how important your needs are) with the expectation that the concomitant nicotine rush shall bring him out of his intense meditation.

Is this corruption?

I will say, 'No'. This is because what you have done is voluntarily (and I stress this word again and again) lubricate the wheels of government so that your file can move from one table to another one five feet away (where the greasing of the gears will once again be repeated).

Of course, it's not as if your file would not be considered if you had not paid the TIPS (which, in case you forgot, stands for 'To Insure Prompt Service') but it might, most unintentionally, get mislabelled, fall out of the window accidentally, or get shoved onto the pile of files furthest inside the cabinet where those horrible termites reside from the times of Lord Curzon. And if that happens, the only person to be blamed would be miserly you because you failed to recognize and appreciate the amount of work that it takes for a pile of papers to move from one table to another, and for an official to just do the job for which the government pays him.

You know what would be corruption? If politicians forced people to pay them money to get things done. Which, I can tell you, almost never happens. People out of their own free will, every year, give millions of rupees to politicians – grateful people like property developers, industrialists and arms salesmen, who just want to ensure 'prompt service' from our elected representatives. If fatter tips get you better service in a restaurant, makes the doorman hold the door open for you for a few seconds longer, and if an extra payment for a business-class ticket gets you more leg-space, a welcome drink and a friendlier smile from the flight attendant, can someone please tell me what is so wrong if politicians help out the people who love them a bit more than the others?

However, one point I need to make before I go on. It is an important one.

As we as a country move beyond the *Dance Dance* disco-age tights, license raj and Johnny Lever, to the 'India Luminant' age (one step beyond 'India Shining' which has become somewhat a cliché and, as has been shown once, a losing political slogan), we need to ascend the rungs of civilization to take our rightful place in the front line of the firmament of nations. This means no more suitcases of cash. That's as passé as asking a video cassette recorder (VCR) for your dowry. Also out are things like weighing politicians in gold (and mashallah, some of our politicians are pound for pound full of the lard of human kindness).

What we need is subtlety. No more David Dhawan. Say hello to Satyajit Ray. Art. Class. Indirection. The hallmark of becoming a 'First World' country is not that money won't change hands (voluntarily, of course) between the political class and other interested parties but that exchange will be done unobtrusively, in a not-in-your-face way.

It's not something that we Indians are totally unaware of. Like, for example, when we gently slip that hundred-rupee note to the office peon asking him to buy 'sahib' a packet of cigarettes. We do that because that's the way it should be done. It's proper. It's gentlemanly. Imagine how ugly it would be if you took a bunch of greasy tenners and hurled it at the officer in question.

It would be shocking. No?

I mean, sure, such 'yeh leh paisa, ab naach chhamiya' behaviour is considered to be par for the course in a house of ill-repute and loose morals. But in a government office – 'Naheen naheen naheen!' Here appearances must be maintained even while the grease is applied in apposite joints.

Following the same principle, our politicians also should obtain their cherry-topped tutti frootis in a roundabout manner. For instance, if a politician owns some stock in a real-estate business (let's call it New Constructions) and then because of some of his well-thought-out policy decisions (like deciding, for instance, to appropriate a park for the purpose of building a shopping mall), New Constructions is found to benefit regularly and consistently, I must say I would call that an example of new-age profiteering and give it an approving thumbs up. I would be even more comfortable if the stock is actually owned not by the politician himself but by a trust with which our politician is very closely associated (i.e. the politician is not directly associated with New Constructions but his son-in-law is). Why? Because of the indirection introduced by the relative, the roundaboutness has become even more roundabout, allowing us to keep up appearances of probity with greater ease.

In contrast, however, if the owner of New Constructions came to the politician's living room and left an envelope of fifty five hundred rupee notes on the coffee table every few months, I would give it a disapproving wag of the finger.

Why? Because taken in the wrong context, that's open for misinterpretation.

Ultimately, you have to accept that 'corruption' is simply a matter of semantics. For instance, in the United States of America the law allows one to influence political decision-makers in a manner that we Indians would wag our fingers at. This legally sanctioned tradition of 'tipping' politicians is known as 'lobbying'.

Make no mistake. Lobbying is serious stuff. Huge lobbying firms exist, many of them comprising ex-legislators, whose job it is to convince the decision-makers in Washington DC to 'support' their clients.

And how is support curried?

Kind of the same way it is done in India – except, like everything in the US, the whole thing is executed by professionals in a thoroughly legal way. Political bigwigs are wined and dined by the lobbyists. They are sent on conferences and junkets and meetings with pressure groups in exotic locales all over the world. Needless to say, even after all this, American politicians are still able to take objective decisions on matters of policy.

Just like their Indian counterparts.

But what about direct contributions to a politician? In the US, they are pretty strict about this – an individual cannot legally contribute more than a certain amount to a political candidate. However, there are certain organizations, with special tax-exempt status called 527s, that can donate to a political cause, with no upper ceiling or disclosure of donations.[5]

Yes, *donate*. The operative word.

Transplanting the American rule to an Indian context, while it would be illegal for you to take a suitcase full of thousand-rupee notes and hand it over to Mantri-sahib's secretary a day before the tenders for the cement supply contract are due to open, it should be perfectly fine for you to be a member of an organization called 'Cementing Industry-Government Relationships', contribute a suitcase full of cash to the said organization, and then for that organization to fund the re-election campaign for Mantri-sahib.

An astute reader will have noticed, by this time, that the trick in eradicating 'corruption' is simply in defining it in a creative way. If only we as a nation are able to push aside

---

5 Referred to as 'soft money.'

our moral intransigence and do the needful in redefining the word and the concept (as the US has done), there is nothing to prevent us from going from Number 83 to Number 18 (USA's rank)[6] in the list of the world's least corrupt nations.

Now would that not be lovely?

6 http://us.rediff.com/money/2003/oct/07corrupt.htm

CHAPTER 8

How to Start Your Own Management Institute

India is fortunate to have several world-renowned management schools whose alumni have, over the years, made an indelible mark for themselves around the globe as captains of industry.

Wait a second. That didn't come out exactly the way I wanted it to. As a matter of fact, it sounded like the typical opening line of a speech at the annual convocation of one of these management schools.

So let me rephrase.

India has several world-renowned management schools whose alumni command astronomical salaries and wield Czar-like influence in today's global corporations.

Needless to say, everyone from Jhoomritalaiya to Jaipur, from Bhootnath Choubey (graduate in Hindi) to Ramanathan Chokhalingam (graduate in electronics) wants to be a member of this super-rich/super-powerful caste of 'management

Brahmins'. Headlines like 'IIMB graduate gets record salary on first day of campus placement' only increase this sense of bechainiya[1] and betaabiyaan.[2]

But in order to take their place in this platinum privileged class, they have to first get admitted to these sought-after management schools. That's much much easier said than done. The entrance tests to these elite places impose unreal demands on a candidate – he/she is expected to fight like Suniel Shetty, kiss like Emraan Hashmi, act like Om Puri, dance like Mithunda and sing like Lata Mangeshkar.

Unfortunately, most people fight like Lata Mangeshkar, kiss like Om Puri, act like Emraan Hashmi, dance like Suniel Shetty and sing like Mithun Chakraborty. This means they do not have an ability to solve mathematical problems extremely fast, nor can they effortlessly make word associations. They get intimidated at group discussions and freeze at personal interviews. As a result they are forever outside, looking in.

Putting my social justice hat on, I think this is grossly unfair. Huge chunks of our population are being denied a shot at their destiny solely on the basis of their inability to solve mathematical problems at insane speeds. (Just like our Indian athletes are unfairly deprived of a chance to win Olympic gold medals because they run slower and jump lower than people from China and the US.)

Since an aptitude for maths and for verbal comprehension is often found to be a function of the environment, the discrimination becomes generational. Some may claim that

---

1 Hindi for uneasiness

2 Hindi for restlessness. Both these words occur in a song from the Hindi movie *Gupt*.

admission to an institute of higher learning is not a question of justice but of merit.

Those who are meritorious deserve preference. It's that simple.

Now normally I totally agree with the principle that 'merit and only merit counts', but since I have put on my social justice hat today I am going to repeat the rhetoric of the reservationists. Namely that merit is just an artificial construct foisted on society by the privileged (in this case, the maths and verbal ability wizards) in order to keep out the unfortunates from the arc-lights of prosperity.

Whew! That's one mouthful.

Someone needs to rectify the situation and bring justice to the downtrodden by making management education available to all.

That someone is me. Which is why I have decided to open a management school myself.

Its stated mission will be to take education to the masses so that those who can attempt only sixteen out of hundred are not deprived of a chance to lord over those that get eighty.

And its unstated mission: to make me a millionaire.

Cynical readers by this time may have figured out why I put on my social justice hat in the preceding paragraphs. I accept it was self-interest that made me do so – perhaps the very same reason why some people oppose the 'merit argument' and support reservation.

In the rest of the chapter, I shall outline winning strategies for starting and running a management institute by telling you how I, a self-declared expert, do it.

At this point of time, you may be tempted to ask why in the first place I am sharing my secrets with you. If these insights are truly valuable, why indeed would I, who wants to be a millionaire, give away my competitive advantage in such a cavalier fashion?

Good question. Now here is the answer.

Altruism.

Surprised that in this day and age, genuine goodness of heart still exists?

Yes it does. It definitely does.

For one, you will find the milk of human kindness in those real estate gurus who show you the path to make a seven-figure income by selflessly revealing insider secrets of buying and selling undervalued properties (once, of course, you buy their videos and instructional manuals that come with a thirty-day money-back guarantee).

You will also find the same milk flowing through the veins of hundreds of Internet heroes who in the space of two hundred pages explain how one can quit their day job and make thousands of dollars just by blogging from your bed or by sending 'focused emails and promotional marketing materials' (some people call this spam). Just like they have. So eager are they to assist you in transforming your life that they will send seven emails to your inbox every day, cleverly bypassing your spam filters.

Of course these people, kind as they are, are surely not the most egregious examples of aggressively altruistic people. The honour of that goes to a select band of men and women who are ready to offer 10 per cent of their wealth of hundreds of millions of dollars if only you help them transfer all their money to your bank.

It was in 1999 that I first came to know that such genuine people exist in the world. I received an e-mail from one lady called Abebe Okele from Nigeria, the late widow of Mr Okele, a high-ranking official in the government who had managed to accumulate (through means that I assumed were not exactly above-board) a hundred million dollars in income. After his death, greedy officials had been hounding Ms Okele, trying to get hold of the money her husband had hidden away. Now Ms Okele was so concerned about her safety that she wanted to transfer her husband's ill-gotten treasure, all hundred million dollars of it, to a bank account in the United States. Since she was surrounded by so many enemies, the *only* person she felt she could trust was me.

Her scheme was simple. She would be glad to wire all her money to my bank account with the understanding that I would, after she escapes from Nigeria, give her money back. As remuneration for my effort, she would give me 10 per cent of her hundred million dollars.

Not that I need money to be helpful, of course. It's in my nature.

Needless to say, I was very flattered at this display of absolute trust from someone who had never met me and did not even know my name. Lesser men than me might be tempted to take the money and then refuse to give it back. Of course I would never do that, but what felt good was that Ms Okele trusted me not to behave thus. In addition, I did like the fact that she was, on her own accord, offering me 10 per cent of her wealth, thus showing that there are some people in this world who know the difference between asking for help and imposing on someone's sense of charity.

Ever since 1999, I have received several such offers (hundreds in fact) with the text of the letter being identical and having similar misspellings but from different people – a deposed dictator from Mali, an oil executive from the Ukraine, the husband of an assassinated politician in Pakistan (whose name I shall not mention for reasons of national security), a diamond miner's daughter from Sierra Leone. I have been amazed how so many people in the world are so ready to part with 10 per cent of their fortunes for almost nothing in return, except of course the privilege of transferring their money to my account. I have been even more amazed that all these people, with nothing common between them, blindly trust me – humble old me.

In a vein of helpfulness similar to what has been detailed above (technically called the 419 scam, which keen readers will note is 1 removed from 420), I now present to you my insights and experiences of how to start a money-making management institute.

CHOOSING A NAME

Some people will tell you that getting the name right is everything. While I cannot tell you for sure whether it helps to become 'Suniel' from 'Sunil' or 'Riteish' from 'Ritesh' or to add several Ks to your name, I can definitely assert that the key to starting a profitable management shop is to choose an apposite name for it. Your name ideally should have at least two of these three words:

1. **Indian**: You want to show prospective students that your institute has an all-India scope – in terms of students, faculty and placements. Even if you have one centre in the mezzanine floor above a grocery store, and your faculty consists of two professors (both of whom stay in the same

building) and the grocery store is where your students are typically placed after graduation, you definitely want the 'Indian' in your name.

2. **Institute**: A crucial word. Nowadays, many favour using the word 'school' as in Harvard Business School, but according to me, in India the word 'school' conjures up images of uniformed school boys and girls with heavy bags on their backs and with water-bottles dangling from their shoulders, sitting on rows of benches with the boring tedium of 'school' life being broken only when one of the students has their ears boxed by a teacher. Surely this is not the mental picture you want prospective students of your management store to conjure up when they come to pick up their prospectuses.

3. **International**: 'Main hoon khiladi, khiladi, international khiladi,' sang Akshay Kumar in the movie *International Khiladi*, thus articulating a desire that all management students have: to be 'international players' in today's integrated world economy. The word 'international' provides an implicit promise of a global education and the prospect of placements in Singapore, Sydney, New York. Or at least Dhaka.

As an example of how these words may be strung together, I use the title of the management institute I propose to start, namely 'Indian Institute of International Dreamers' shortened as I3D.

Readers are asked to note how I have used 'I3D' instead of 'IIID'. The reasons are obvious: pronouncing IIID makes you sound like a stammerer while I3D has a cool, sexy and futuristic feel to it.

A good question to ask now is why I have used the word 'dreamers' in the name. The answer to this provides us the perfect transition into the next section which is...

CHOOSING A CONCEPT

This is perhaps one of the most important things to get right – what management-type people would call 'branding'. In this exercise, your task is to distinguish your product from its competitors so that what you are trying to sell 'stands out' from the rest.

In the world of management stores, successful branding depends critically on coming up with an appropriate 'hook' that encapsulates the founding principle of your institution, the reason for its existence. (The actual reason is to make you money, of course, but play along with me here.)

Important point: Adopting an ambitious 'hook' does not necessarily mean that your institute has to do anything different. You just have to appear to be distinctive.

Let me explain the concept of a 'hook' with my own example. Recall the name I have chosen for my management institute: Indian Institute of International Dreamers. The hook here, as you may have guessed, is the word 'dreamers'. The way the hook is fledged out is like this.

The big names, the Indian Institutes of Management and such like, teach you management. Sure. They have been more or less following the same paradigm for decades now – teach marketing, finance, economics and a gaggle of such subjects before letting their graduates loose on the world with a degree and a headful of jargon.

What do these graduates do then? They make twenty lakhs a year. Maybe in a few years, they make forty lakhs a year.

But is that all there is to management education? Should the success of institutes be measured by the pay packets of its graduates?

Or should we be asking instead:

'Have the graduates of these prestigious institutes changed the world?'

Well, have they? The answer is a resounding 'no'.

While a few may have brought in a revolution or a half, most of them have done little except prepare reports, make presentations, attend meetings, shout at subordinates and pocket a fat bonus.

The big lacuna in management education, we feel, is that students are not taught to dream. So that when they graduate they may know how to valuate complex derivatives but know absolutely nothing about imagining and dreaming.[3]

Many years ago, Isaac Newton saw an apple fall, like so many others before him.

But unlike everyone else, Newton dreamt.

Big.

The world changed.

Now that's vision.

That's what I3D will teach you.

Bill Gates had a dream, Martin Luther King had a dream, Mungeri Lal had a dream.

Dreamers bring revolutions. They create institutions. They build nations.

But how shall you dream if you are not taught to?

---

3 Some may say that valuing derivatives is nothing but imagining and dreaming but I would not like to believe so.

Remember that without training and discipline all that you will have are wet dreams. In the end, what you will amount to will be exactly what happens to wet dreams. Frustration. Nyet, nada, zilch, zero. Even with your fancy PGDMs and MBAs.

That's where I3D steps in. We shall teach you how to dream big – to dream about your future, to dream about your job and to dream about ways to change the world.

The astute reader will have noticed how I have branded my institute, in the process justifying its name and also thrown a few barbs at my competition. Needless to say, I now have people's attention, especially of those who could not get into the top management institutes and are, as a result, licking their paws. The genius of this pitch is that through it I am providing them a way to convince themselves that by studying at I3D, they are getting better education than they would get at the more established institutes, where they could not, as you recall, get in.

However, the true impact of the pitch can be realized only if it is delivered by the right person. In other words, the message here is as important as the messenger.

ACT THE PART

The number of murgas (sorry, students) your pitch will be able to snare (sorry, enroll) will depend critically on the founder of the institute, and his own personal credibility as a guru in the management market.

To be honest, perhaps the most difficult part of this business is creating one's own reputation as a management guru. (I personally am in the process of doing this myself.) That is because the market for self-promoted experts is highly competitive and there is no ready formula for fame. Personal achievement is definitely not a prerequisite. The ability to appear knowledgeable certainly is.

As an owner, there however exists another alternative to becoming a guru yourself. If you can convince an already established guru, through financial and other incentives, to plug your institute's philosophy in his books and public engagements then you are on solid ground.

There is however a long-term problem with the above approach. Gurus that endorse you today have no obligation to keep on doing so, once one of your competitors makes an even more 'convincing' argument to him/her.

The most important defining criterion for a management guru is that all his statements have to sound very deep and be delightfully vague. Deep and vague statements have an instinctive aura of profoundness about them that instantaneously impresses.

This is what I call the 'Emperor's new clothes' syndrome. This derives its name from the famous fairy tale where even though the citizens see that the emperor is naked, they applaud his clothes because they have been told the clothes are such that only the wise can see them.

This is, no doubt, a very powerful socio-psychological instrument which any management guru worth his name has to take advantage of. The entire avant-garde art industry owes its profits to it. If people did not go 'waah waah' over a blank canvas with a dab of red paint on it or over a soiled toilet seat in an exhibition just because they have been told that this is high art, where would modern artists be?

Deep-sounding words make the founder of the institute sound like a visionary. The vagueness is important because people expect management gurus to be somewhat like religious mystics, i.e. speak in parables and riddles with each of their sentences open to multiple interpretations. This expectation is like manna from heaven for the gurus because it enables them to go through their entire lives without saying one thing that is original or is of value, as long as they are able to fry it deep in the oil of obfuscated profoundness.

To get further insight into how they operate, I asked a very successful management guru, a dear friend of mine, Neil Chris B (real name: Neelbaran Krishnachandra Batabyal) about his modus operandi. This is what he told me, after I had plied him with a few drinks. Needless to say, since I wanted him to tell me the real truth, I forgot to tell him that he was being taped.

As an established 'guru' myself, I have perfected the art of vagueness. I confess that all my speeches are almost exactly the same. They consist of a laundry list of the hoariest of management clichés that I have collected from reading about fifteen management books.

However, what I almost always change is what I call the 'delivery vehicle'.

For example, if I want to appear a master of the Japanese school of management (was very fashionable in the '80s, now a bit out of style), I will drop samurai metaphors (a weakly managed team becomes a group of 'ronins' – a ronin is a master-less samurai) and rely on Zen sayings ('The torch of doubt and chaos, this is what the sage steers by' or 'No yesterday, no tomorrow, and no today') to sound deep. I find that nothing works better in this context than to recite the odd haiku, even when the haiku has nothing to do with the cliché you are currently explaining.

If I am doing an Indian management themed thing, the 'delivery vehicle' changes accordingly as I fall back on Sanskrit slokas, replacing the Zen sayings with random quotes from the Upanishads. Sometimes I make up the Sanskrit as I go. I have yet to find one sucker who can tell the difference.

If I realize that the audience is interested in the way the Chinese do it, I use Lao-Tzu ('Therefore the manager is guided by what he feels and not by what he sees. He lets go of that and chooses this') and the obligatory Sun Tzu Art of War metaphors which I find go down extremely well.

Then if I see the audience has a fetish for the American way (this is currently out of fashion), I become a cross between a motivational speaker and an evangelist, liberally using American sporting metaphors and pacing the stage, trying to work the audience into a nervous frenzy.

And finally sometimes people just want to get away from work and have fun on the company tab. But they do not know how to make it look like a legitimate corporate expense. I then step in with a four-day programme wherein I promise to teach team-building, innovation and strategic decision-making in a very 'out-of-the-box' fashion. I then take the fatcats to a nice resort and stand like a kindergarten teacher supervising them as they play 'hide-and-seek', 'dog and bone', 'tug of war' and similarly challenging games. This is not as easy as it sounds since I continuously have to make up some interesting story to explain how playing these games in a hill-station will make their company a 'leaner, meaner' organization. Not that I have to try too hard, since my students, having a paid holiday courtesy the poor shareholders, are as easily convinced as second graders are about the existence of Santa Claus.

In passing, one thing I find extremely popular with all my audiences is talking about management ethics, which I think goes down best with

> *my 'Indian-style management' themed talk because I can then make a nice-sounding cocktail with Indian philosophy, karma, cosmic balance. It's ironic because I look around in my audience and find many captains of industry, known for following what I can politely call their 'sharp practices'. I think that the way their mind works is that they feel that attending a talk about management ethics washes away their sins, as if they are visiting a temple. Not that I mind, of course. I always ask for thirty thousand extra for the module on ethics – a payment I take in cash because of income tax considerations.*

THE BROCHURE

Now we come to the important part. The brochure. This has to be crafted most carefully. Positives have to be exaggerated. If none exist, then they have to be made up. Needless to say, negatives have to be suppressed.

One thing I always repeat to myself, five times every day and one more time if I feel myself slipping, is that as an owner I am only interested in the profit I make and not actually in the quality of the education imparted or the employment-worthiness of those who study at my shop. This is why I always, and I repeat, always, ask before every investment the question 'Would this make my institute more sellable?' rather than 'Would this actually help my students?'

The guiding principle behind successfully selling I3D is to understand what my target audience i.e. prospective students expect to see from a premier management institute.

Expectation 1: A private management institute should look good.

When prospective students or their parents (Mr Moneybags) come to my institute to take a walk-through, I spare no effort to make sure that they be impressed by the learning environment I provide – the spacious buildings, the modern architecture, the Japanese gardens, the overall landscaping, the Olympic-size swimming pool, the gymnasium and squash courts, the working air-conditioning (I make sure this always works: rich kids hate hot rooms), the futuristic lecture halls (which may fancily be called e-kul – electronic Gurukul) and the diffused lighting in the halls. This is a crucial part of what I call the 'creation of a positive mind-space' as research has shown that an automatic association is made between the quality of the facilities and the quality of education.

Expectation 2: As a student I expect an 'international' education.

Regardless of whether you have the word 'international' in your title, students nowadays expect to get a global MBA, one that has instant name recognition in the hallowed halls of industry – everywhere from New York to Nandigram, from London to Lahore. Since they pay several lakhs a semester, my job is to make sure that they keep labouring under the (mis)apprehension (at least till they have finished paying all their instalments) that the education they are getting from my institute will lead to international employers grovelling at their doorsteps saying, 'Please please work for me.'

The façade of internationality can be maintained through the adoption of a variety of devices. For one, the brochure could list addresses of foreign campuses of the institute along with professionally taken pictures of the same. If this sounds as something beyond your budget, worry not. The campuses do not necessarily have to exist. Put some random addresses and phone numbers from the London or Prague phonebook and list them as the locations of your offshore campuses. Take some pictures of nice-looking buildings with awe-inspiring façades (second time we are using this word in the paragraph) and put these right next to the addresses. (Make sure the brochure is printed on the best quality of photographic paper.)

This ruse, in itself, is not sufficient and might fool some of the people some of the time but not all of the people all of the time. That is why actual collaborations with several foreign universities have to be established so that the programme appears truly global. While it is unlikely that the big names of the management education industry will partner with you unless your pockets are as deep as the Mariana Trench, there are several other lesser players with whom a mutually beneficial agreement may be worked out.

For instance, I3D has negotiated memoranda of understandings (profit-sharing) with four institutes (one in Glasgow, one in Aruba, one in Morocco and another in Timbuctoo) such that students who enrol in the I3D 'Milky Way MBA' programme (other schools have Global MBA programmes, we at I3D have even greater scope) may take credits at each of these schools. Because of these tie-ins, we write in our brochure that I3D's MBAs are 'inter-galactically recognized', though honestly I have no idea what that means.

At this point of time, let me get you in on a dirty secret, one that took me much effort to figure out. Many of my students at I3D have joined management school just to have a 'good time' while pretending to their parents to be under severe academic pressure. My job is to help them keep up that appearance.

As an example, if someone walks up to their Dad and says, 'Daddio, I need some money to go to Amsterdam for the summer with a group of friends,' Dad is most likely to plant a few quick kicks up the said person's backside and shout, 'Smoke weed on your own dime.'

However, if the same person tells his dad, 'Dad, I finished top 5 per cent of my class in International Finance. And you know what! I3D has selected me to represent India for the world's premier summer school on derivatives pricing at Amsterdam. I3D will pay 100 per cent of my summer school fees – I just need money to buy the tickets and make hotel reservations. I3D will do all the bookings themselves,' Dad is likely to feel so proud of his achieving son that not only will he pay up, but he will also grandly announce to the neighbourhood, 'My darling son is the only person in the country who has won this prestigious scholarship to a summer school in Amsterdam.' [Note: The son never said 'only person'. Dad assumed this.]

What I do is to work out a deal with one of the hundreds of 'exclusive' summer schools that are held each year in Europe wherein you get a discounted rate, if you can guarantee a certain number of attendees. The cost of the '100 per cent scholarship' I am giving to the student is actually included in his course fees and so it's not as if I am actually having to pay for even this concessional rate from my own pocket. Since I will be making the travel arrangements for quite a few students, I have another chance to make some money by negotiating group rates with travel agents. So when an ecstatic student gives me the equivalent of $5000 for his summer school attendance, I give the travel agency $3000 and keep the rest, thus creating a perfect confluence between myself and my student's professional goals – both of us profit.

Expectation 3: Students expect the best syllabus and the best faculty.

Dealing with the syllabus issue is the easiest. I go online, point my browser to the course webpages of the Top 10 business schools in the world, and copy down the syllabus of each course and yes that becomes your syllabus. I always remember that the instructor is not obliged to follow the official syllabus nor is he/she expected to even understand it.

Getting big-name faculty is slightly more challenging. The quick and dirty – or should I say, very dirty – way is to just write down the names of famous professors as faculty without telling them. Later, if students raise questions as to why they never see him/her showing up, you can always say that Dr So-and-So will not be available for this semester. Warning: doing this for too many years in succession may lead to your bluff being called.

A more sustainable arrangement for a stellar faculty roster is to make financial arrangements with big-name professors such that their names may legitimately be used as faculty. Of course since famous professors from MIT and Stanford are not actually going to become full-time faculty (if they do, they remain famous no longer) at I3D, all that I can get them to do is to fly down for two lectures a semester.

This works out sweet for the famous professors, many of whom are of Indian origin, who typically do whirlwind lecture tours of different management institutes (they are guest faculty at each of them) and rake in a pretty penny, like rock bands on concert trips.

Of course getting 'live' faculty for all the courses is beyond my budget (famous people charge a lot!). Hence I often go for pre-recorded video lectures given by famous management faculty.

You may be thinking right now: if the star faculty is so perfunctorily invested in the institute, who does the bulk of the teaching at I3D? Who grades the exams? Who answers student's doubts?

The answer is simple: ex-students. Alumni of I3D are the ideal instructors. They know the drill, they know the philosophy. The only reason they are working for I3D is because their dreams did not find acceptance in the job market. This means they have no other employment choices. Ergo they will work cheap. Of course they cannot be given credit for teaching the course as their names look bad on the brochure.

There is another advantage in hiring one's own students. Even though we cannot mention them as faculty, a student hired by I3D implies a successful placement. This bolsters our placement stats (after all a 'placement' does not need to imply an 'external placement') and makes us that much more 'sexy' for prospective education-seekers.

Expectation 4: Students expect great campus placements.

Placement is the reason why they joined in the first place. To become part of the jet-set crowd. The first step towards that is their first job, the one that they get from on-campus interviews.

Now once the students are enrolled, I just tell them that our job centre believes in the maxim: 'God helps those who help themselves.' But for obvious reasons, we cannot put this down in the brochure as it may be misunderstood.

One of the first things that prospective students look at is the name of companies who have come on campus and the percentage of students who were recruited there. The 'percentage of students placed' metric is gamed by our policy of hiring ex-students as unofficial instructors. If the number of students who have not received any job offer is more than the number of instructors we need, I just give them an appointment letter and keep them 'on the bench'. When they are on the bench, they get no salary but are technically employed. This works out to my benefit. Why? I think you got it figured out.

As to the list of companies, any and every company that has ever hired an I3D alumni is put on the list, regardless of whether they came to the campus or hired a person for a set of skills for which I3D is not responsible (like if a student gets a job modeling underwear). Sometimes, when times are bad, I just put any company I fancy on the list. Anything, they say, is fair in love, war and in getting students to enrol in your management school.

Expectation 5: Students want to study in a high-ranked institute.

Rank, like size, matters. That is because the rank is one number that encapsulates an institution's reputation like nothing else. When Mother 1 meets Mother 2 at the kitty party, you can be sure that all they care about is whose daughter goes to the school with the higher rank.

This is one place where the non-elite institutes are at a chronic disadvantage because the big boys have a brand reputation built over the years and consequently a permanent monopoly on the top rankings. So how do we at I3D correct this imbalance?

Simple. In India, there is no single accepted authority for management school rankings. Most of the ranking initiatives are run by magazines/newspapers. So, for twenty media outlets, there are twenty different rankings. The methodology by which they rank institutes is also different and most of the time non-transparent.

This state of affairs is most fortunate for people like us. All that I do is to find a media entity ready to be influenced. The arrangement is simple: I put full-page advertisements in their newspaper and buy ad-space on their website. In return, we are guaranteed a high place in their management school rankings. This endorsement of quality, I then make sure, is prominently displayed in our brochure and press releases.

Remember, however, that your rivals are playing this game too. Sometimes I am approached by a magazine/newspaper for data regarding my institute for their rankings, an organization which I know has already committed to a similar financial arrangement with a competitor.

I promptly refuse to take part in their ranking process. I then send a letter from my lawyer to the magazine concerned telling them to prominently carry the disclaimer 'I3D refused to take part in the ranking process' at the bottom of the article. Or else.

Expectation 6: The institute should be an accredited entity.

Accreditation in India is a process I do not much care for. After all, why should the opinion of a few people representing the Government of India matter? If the government knew anything about management, you would expect the country to be better run, wouldn't you? Whatever respect I had for the government accreditation agency vanished the day they refused to give I3D that blessed scrap of paper. So I said: who needs a licence from the government to dream in any case? Better off without one.

Yes, I know. I am a libertarian.

My tie-ups with international management institutes solve the accreditation problem. Now I just let the students assume that the degree we hand out has the sanction of these foreign universities. They are happy thinking that they are getting foreign degrees sitting in India. And I am happy simply because they are happy.

To be legally above board, we do mention that our degrees are still not recognized in India but for reasons of space, we are forced to accommodate that caveat at the very bottom of our brochure, in a font size so small that even ants would struggle to read it with a magnifying glass.

By this time, I am sure that most of you have got a decent enough idea of how to proceed towards starting your own management institute. Remember, this is not just an exercise in self-aggrandizement but a holy war to break the monopoly of the elite institutes on the dispensation of MBA degrees, to bring true social justice to corporate governance, to wipe away the tears of those who struggle with numbers or are a few seconds too late to think of an answer to questions like 'Sell yourself'.

Now go forth and multiply. Your earnings, that is.

CHAPTER 9

An Indian Wedding

When I was young, and even after I was not that young, I would ask my parents to tell me about their wedding. For some reason that was scarcely fathomable they never seemed to care talking about it, brushing off my patient queries with a 'It's so long ago' and 'Don't remember much of it'. I felt it odd that they would forget such an important day of their lives though I do know that my dad is forgetful at times.

Once I myself got married, I realized the truth.

The reason why they did not remember was because they wanted to forget.

That's because Indian weddings are torture, torture of the first order. Of course, being a construct of an advanced civilization and culture, its insidious way of meting out punishment is, at first glance, not in contravention of the Geneva Conventions. Which perhaps explains why Dick Cheney and other bigwigs in the US Republican administration, if they had been a bit less ethnocentric, would have realized the potential of Indian marriage rituals to crack up the toughest of Al Qaeda nuts, without getting into 'water boarding' and other controversial instruments of information gathering.

Of course this realization of Indian marriage ceremonies being torture on the groom and bride would be something that would dawn on me only after I had gone through its grind. Before that, just like many innocent people, I had an immense fascination for weddings and looked forward eagerly to my own.

This was not due to the inherent appeal of the pomp and the grandeur of an Indian wedding. Nor was this because of a romantic desire for *Hum Mar Chuke Sanam*-style 'aankhon ki gustakhiyan maaf ho' nokjhok.

Putting it very simply, I wanted to be the groom. You have to believe me when I say that this was not because the brides caught my fancy.[1] The reason was that I wanted to be at the centre of attention, the cynosure of all eyes. I had seen how everybody fretted and fussed over the groom, how for a few days the world was there to attend to him and indulge his whims.

So I decided to get married. How I met my wife-to-be and what happened before the wedding is not relevant to this chapter. More precisely, it would take quite a few more pages to finish that story. Even more precisely, I do not exactly remember.

What, however, I can say is that it was a 'love marriage'. And no, it was not one of those pansy 'arranged-cum-love' marriages.

---

1 I am lying about this – the brides were one of the main reasons.

Sofa-cum-bed I understand.

But what the hell is an arranged-cum-love-marriage?

I mean isn't it a contradiction in terms? Or what your English professor would call an oxymoron?

Well, what an arranged-cum-love-marriage actually means is that after hours of browsing through albums of assorted beauties and then following that up with frenetic scraps on Orkut pleading for friendship, you have come up with nothing. Faced with the possibility of eternal bachelorhood or a meaningful relationship with one's hand, you have been forced to let your parents step in to find a 'homely, convent-educated' girl of 'fairish or wheatish' complexion.

And now you are too ashamed to accept that fact and have to put a veneer of 'love' to cover up for the essentially 'arranged' nature. Almost like the way the phrase 'competitive cricket' covered up the essentially fixed nature of many matches in the roaring 1990s.

Come on guys. Let's face it.

Once all the fluff is got rid of, an arranged marriage boils down to the BBB factor: the Bigger and Better Bet. Guys go for the prettiest Aishwarya lookalike they can find while girls go for Mr Moneybags. After all, that's all you can judge before an arranged marriage. And oh yes, the Hindi filmi criteria of khandan. Quite forgot that. If the richer get the prettier, then I wonder where that white-hot ethereal ideal of love enters the equation. I also find the term 'love marriage' rather curious. It precludes 'arranged' marriages from having love in it!

Arranged Marriage Cliché 1:

Question to her: Will you be able to adjust with my parents? My unmarried sister? We have always been a joint family.

What she says: Of course.

What she thinks: Mama's boy. Belongs on the sets of a Sooraj Barjatya movie. Strike off list.

Arranged Marriage Cliché 2:

Question to him: Have you ever had girlfriends before? I mean of the special kind...

What he says: Of course, many. But they meant nothing to me. I want to settle down now.

What he thinks: Hope she doesn't ask for more information. I don't want her to know she is the first woman I have been out with, despite my best efforts.

Arranged Marriage Cliché 3:

What he says: I want someone to share my life in the US.

What he means: I want someone to help shovel the snowwalk 'cause, God, it hurts doing it alone.

Enough of digressions! When I got married I was a PhD student, a class of people also known as 'God's forgotten children', grinding away in foreign climes for a degree. I got down from the plane and immediately I felt different and cared for. There was my would-be wife, her parents and her brother standing to receive me with a bouquet of flowers! Now in all my life no one had ever received me with flowers, which I always thought was a God-given privilege for ministers and captains of industry. And here I was, humble graduate student, alighting from the plane after twenty-three hours of flying cattle-class, in the middle seat between a snoring uncle and a 300-lb aunty, being greeted with a full bouquet of fresh, real flowers. Oh, the importance!

It was not long after that I realized how things were going to be very different from now on. Not that I needed any help. Because no sooner had I plonked down onto my comfortable sofa back home than mother kept on repeating how I was going to become someone else's. And that my loyalties would change: 'A son is a son till he has a wife. A daughter is a daughter all her life' and all that jazz.

Of course Ma wanted to be reassured, repeatedly and with all sincerity, that unlike all the other newly-married sons of her friends, my loyalties to my parents were NOT going to change and that I would always remember who brought me up. Needless to say, I hugged her: 'Oh Ma, of course I am still your baby.' [Dad does not much care for this sentimentality. He would be only too glad to get rid off me for good.]

Lest some quick-to-judge readers are already shaking their heads morosely and whispering 'spineless' under their breath, let me make things absolutely clear.

I am, by no stretch of the term, a 'mama's boy', and my mother assures me that is the case.

The reason I was pandering to Ma was strategic, guided by the same Machiavellian principle the government follows when it drops corruption charges against certain political power centres before a no-confidence motion. The simple fact was that the wedding was not yet over and there was no denying that I could not piss her off at this stage. Or get her overly sentimental. She is the main organizer around the house. My dad and I are no good at the stuff.

God knows why people think that daughters-in-law make the son become detached from his parents. Well, perhaps they do sometimes. But in my case there was little to worry about. I was already sufficiently detached and ungrateful. So my parents knew there was not much to blame anyone else for. I had done pretty much and said everything there was to be said before I even thought of getting married. So, if anything, I was going to improve, and my wife would get the credit.

Damn. I am digressing again. Anyway, the preparations for the wedding were on in full swing. Being a lazy guy with not much sense of responsibility, I let my mother do most of the work. After all, since I was her only child, I did not want to deprive her of the happiness of arranging everything herself. That would have been a most selfish thing to do. So I profitably used whatever time I could get to spend with my to-be-wife and be generally up to 'no good'.

But there was something I just could not avoid. And that was the shopping. Shopping is something that has always been a pain even in the best of times. It's even less fun when it's your in-laws who are taking you out for shopping.

First of all, the very fact that they are buying you stuff is deeply embarrassing. Then for most of the time you don't really know what to say, leading to long awkward silences and fidgeting.

For instance when mother-in-law asks: 'What type of shoes would you like to buy?' you become acutely conscious of the price. Remember you cannot just walk up and start looking at the tags. If I was getting my daughter married and I saw my would-be damaad looking intently at the price stickers I would say, 'No no, don't bother about the price. Just tell us the one you like,' but I would be thinking, 'That bum is going to buy the most expensive one possible on our tab.' Conscious of how

I would think if I were in their position, I stay as away from the shoe-rack as possible.

But then I do need to make a choice. Cannot stand looking at the ceiling all day. If you go 'unbranded' even then there is a problem. First of all, your in-laws might think you are patronizing them. This may lead to further periods of tense silence. Second, if the thing is really hideous looking, do remember you will have to wear it for many years. Else your wife is going to say, 'How come you never wear what my parents gave you? Think you are too good for them, right?'

So you are in essence damned if you do and damned if you don't.

As if that was not enough of a dharm-sankat, my in-laws took me shopping with a distant relative of theirs who was their version of a wedding planner. Jennifer Lopez he definitely was not, and I am not just referring to his posterior![2] I remember him going to one shop and telling the guy who brings out the clothes: 'Bring out the best stuff you have. Our son-in-law wants only the very best.' Yikes! That was really the last thing I wanted to hear. Obviously, with such company, all I could think of was when this ordeal was going to end.

And when our family did the shopping, Ma took over. (As my dad would say: 'So what's new?') She made us hotfoot all over Kolkata looking for better deals. So there we were spreading out to the farthest corners of the city, raiding the seedy bylanes, scanning the forgotten New Market alleys. And while mother-in-law and daughter-in-law were bonded

---

2 Jennifer Lopez acted in a horrendous movie called *The Wedding Planner*, a movie so syrupy that even Yash Chopra would say 'Kuch zyada ho gaya'.

by this shared love of tireless shopping, I kept looking at paint dry on walls.

My parents had of course started the invitation process a long time before I had arrived. A little history. My dad (like me) likes to set trends. When his father died, he set a trend by not shaving off his hair; a gesture that I believe did not go down well with the traditionalists in our family. As you might have guessed by now, my dad does not believe in anything. Including the fact that I am his son!

This time around, my dad decided to set another precedent. He decided that he was not going to everyone's place personally and invite him or her. Instead, he would choose to rely on that marvellous modern invention – the telephone. Going to people's houses personally and inviting them for one's son's wedding was a fine thing to do in those days when men and women had time to chew paan and eat five-course meals. But in today's 'time is money' world this concept no longer makes any sense. None at all. So Baba decided to dispense with it.

He compromised a bit, however, and personally invited only those people who were senior to him. This was a smart move. Baba, being no spring chicken, did not have too many people senior to him who were alive. That means not too many places to visit.

But of course some people, who shall remain nameless (in case they are reading the book, yes, we know who you are) got offended at the fact that Baba had not 'personally' gone to their houses and invited them. They naturally took this to be a personal affront.

What's the matter, people? The important thing is that you have been invited. It's not how you have been invited.

But no. You just have to make this a matter of ego. Somehow there is a belief that just because someone's son or daughter is getting married, they should be obligated to everyone. Ergo they have to drop in personally, the more inconvenient it is for them the better, and suitably stroke people's egos.

Ma had a good explanation: it's because people love us so much and so aggressively that they want us to visit them.

Right. They love us so much that if we do not visit, their love reveals itself in the form of tongues wagging and disapproving nods of the head.

This love we can surely do without.

Before the wedding, one of the big occasions for running around and barking orders and getting people fretting and fuming is the Bengali tradition of 'totto shajano'. That is, taking gifts packed in such a pretty way that no one would want to open them. A mountain of wasted effort I would say. But then again, so is marriage!

It was rather fun, however, especially since I was not doing it. My aunts did it interspersing their efforts with attempts to pull my leg. It's all part and parcel of the general gaiety (I use it in the old sense of the term as in, 'Let's have a gay time in the woods') and I took it gamely. Except that I have heard these same gags, like millions of times.

And such lame ass ones too.

Chillers like, 'Oh thinking about your wife?'.

No, of course not. I am thinking of my ex-girlfriend and how she 'achchha silaah diya mere pyar ka'-ed me a few years ago. Of course I am thinking about my wife. What's their problem? I know they are trying to be friendly. But somehow when you are missing your wife (you are not supposed to see her for a few days before the marriage or something to that effect), being pestered on the issue is like having a rough shoe continuously rub against a toe blister. Not fun.

Then the day of the marriage arrives. This is when I realized that the whole affair was not a question of making the groom feel important. It was a matter of being made the punch-line of a huge joke. I felt, not for the first time in the last few days, that I was trapped in a classic Govinda comedy in which nothing made sense.

The day for me was to start at the crack of dawn. My first act was to taste some yogurt. Now why would eating yogurt before sunrise have anything to do with solemnizing a social contract between two people?

Let me give you the official reason. By tasting that yogurt, I am somehow paying tribute to my ancestors. Who the hell thought of this anyway? What does yogurt have to do with ancestors, who may be lactose intolerant for all I know?

Of course, I did no such thing. Woke up pretty late, had a dash of yogurt. According to custom I was not supposed to eat for the day but Geneva Conventions specifically forbid Prisoners of War (POWs) from being deprived of 2000 calories a day. So I ate, naturally.

Waking up, I had to sit in on the 'nannimukh' ceremony, which I was told was once again an invocation of my ancestors. I am sure my ancestors would have been silently screaming, 'No no, don't do it and further pollute the gene pool. Do you really want another copy of yourself?'

The ceremony seemed sort of fun. What I noticed, putting my software engineer hat on, was that the mantras seemed to be like parameterized functions. The text of the mantra, i.e. the function body, remained the same while the function kept being called with different names of gods as input parameters.

There were a bevy of fruits all spread out with a prominence of big bananas.

Just an observation.

After that ceremony was the 'gaaye holud' ceremony. This is the morning striptease show where I am supposed to stand bare-torso in front of a gaggle of middle-aged women (aunts and neighbours) while I am smeared with turmeric and then bathed. Traditionally, this is supposed to happen under the cool shade of some tree, but best of luck for finding a tree in the city of Kolkata.

Not that even if a tree was found I was going to allow myself to stand out in the open, shirtless like Salman Khan, and have water poured down my spine. After all, this was my marriage for God's sake, not some public spectacle. Plus I don't really have the physique to display my torso – a Greek god I am not by any means! An elephant being washed by their mahouts would be a more pleasing sight than me with water droplets streaming down my upper body.

So in order to spare the cosmos of this sorry sight, I stood in the relative privacy of the balcony while four banana leaves representing four trees were placed at four corners. Then in the midst of this sparse vegetation, I stood covering my torso with a towel, with my eyes telling the assembled lady-folk, 'Chod do towel zamana kya kahega.' Not heeding my silent cry, they savagely smeared me with turmeric. While all this happened, the cameramen and video photographers made sure those moments of embarrassment would be enshrined forever.

After that was over, there was nothing left for me to do. For the time being. The house, of course, was full of people all busy and running about and shouting orders to no one in particular. All except me, that is. I knew that it was going to be a long night (Nah, not in the way you are thinking!) and I needed to keep myself rested and lucid. Time to catch forty winks.

But not before one more exercise in public humiliation. Bengali grooms wear a headdress called a 'topor', a sartorial attachment that most closely resembles a dunce cap (I wonder why!). Now it seems I was to have my head measured so that they could buy one that fitted. Yes you heard that right. Have my head measured. So someone took a measuring tape and started to do the needful with occasional exclamations of 'This is huge!' while I resisted the urge to shout out, like the John Malkovitch character in *Being John Malkovitch*: 'It's my head!'

On the subject of marriage gear, the topor was not my principal area of concern. What I was actually worried about was the dhoti (pronounced dhuti) – the carefully folded cloth, staple of Bengali weddings, which would be covering the business end of my anatomy.

The dhoti is a garment which reveals more than it conceals and has an unfortunate tendency of revealing the inside of your thighs and other assorted attachments if you are not very careful. Even more dangerous, it is held up by a wonder of knot tying. One false move, and you were likely to be exposed and that too on the biggest night of your life.

Now you would say, 'Indians have worn the dhoti for ages, what is your problem?' The fact is I do not know how to tie a dhoti. So if the curtains came down, not only would I be in my bare essentials in front of the whole world, I would also have to wait for someone else to tie it for me. In short, a potential nightmare just waiting to happen.

In the days of yore, the dhoti would be tied with much fanfare by the barber.[3] This barber is a rather unique part of

---

3 If the word 'barber' is offensive to you, like it was for the people who protested against *Billu Barber*, please replace the word 'barber' with 'hairdresser' in your mind. No offence is intended.

traditional Bengali weddings. There are supposed to be two of them – one from each side. In order to get married, you had to, at one time, go long distances, over rough roads often reduced to muddy quagmires by the monsoon rains. After such a harrowing journey you needed someone to freshen the groom, give him a shave, clean him up and in general make him look moderately decent. So a barber, who was the closest one could get to a make-up artist in those days, was a necessity.

In the twenty-first century, in the age of beauty parlours and exfoliation treatments, the barber exists only as a quaint relic of the past. I have mentioned before my dad's courageous Raja Rammohan Ray-style departures from tradition. Therefore he took the bold step of having no barber from our side. Maybe he did not shake the structure of Bengali society with this one, but it surely saved us from having one more non-entity to tip. The downside of this was my dad and my uncle had to tie up my dhoti.

There is yet another bit of fun in Bengali weddings. For some strange reason, you have to change everything once you go to the girl's house. And that includes the dhoti. Traditionally it is something that is more or less done in front of everyone with some thin piece of cloth separating the hero from the ogling masses.

I had made it clear that I was not going to put up with that public disrobing. I needed room and personal space to change. Except that with me unable to tie a dhoti properly, someone had to be with me to do the needful! I was apprehensive about the whole thing – would my wife's family remember to set aside a room for me or would they just say, 'We are all closing our eyes.' More importantly, with total lack of control over the dhoti, I felt as helpless as a child who would need an adult to change his diaper, should he soil it.

That was however not the end of my problems with the costume. The silk kurta I wore (called punjabi, for some strange reason, in Bangla) felt like newspaper rubbing against my skin, making my back itch as a result. On top of that someone came and painted floral designs using chandan (sandalwood paste) on my forehead while I sat still.

Painted like a flower pot and looking like a daisy, I completed the get-up by wearing the topor for which I had been measured. Thus bedecked, I waited for the car to come and take me away.

Soon would-be-Mrs's uncle came as the representative of the bride's side to escort me to the wedding hall. There was the blowing of conch shells, some hugs, some pranaams and I was given a grand send-off.

Lots of smiles.

Lots of photos.

Please look this way.

Yes, over here also.

Hold these flowers.

No no, not like that. Light reflecting off your specs. Just roll your eyes – yes, just right!

The evening was off to a flying start.

The car that had arrived to pick me up was a white Ambassador so covered with flowers that the driver would have no other choice than to drive using his Jedi force, since there was no way he would have a clear line of sight.

Not that I was worried about that. My immediate concern was to get into the car with my rustling kurta, my jiggling dhoti, the heavy flower garland hanging like an albatross round my neck, and of course that sky-high topor, all without having a wardrobe malfunction. Things were not made easy by the jostling crowd shouting advice and the priest asking me to do some sort of wacky Amitabh Bachchan-style foot shuffling just before I left, supposedly to scare off evil spirits.

I think he was just having a little fun at my expense. But then why single him out? Everyone was in on the joke.

After half an hour of being driven by the driver's instincts, we arrived. My advent in the bride's house was greeted by a round of conch blowing and a disembodied voice shouting: 'Mahabali gadadhari mahaveer padhaar rahe hain.'

Ok, I made that up but some of my wife's young sisters did put a rose in my hand. Thus decked in my dhoti, kurta and with a rose in hand, I felt I looked more like Chunni-babu in *Devdas* on a night out on town rather than a groom come to solemnize a lifelong bond of love and respect.

I had never understood why celebrities push the camera away and act all angry and distraught when the videocameras catch them in a public function. I finally got it on my wedding day. There were two sets of video crews and still photographers – one hired by our side and one from their side. (Yes, I know I know after marriage there is no 'ours' and no 'theirs'. But this was before.) It seems that the videocamera guys had failed to record my arrival (or as the front-stallers call it, the entrance) the first time around. So I had to redo it. That means I had to get back into the car, be handed the rose once again and basically do everything I just did.

Now, I am by no means a moody celebrity. As a matter of fact I am as much hungry for video attention as those who, when they see a TV reporter, try to jump over his shoulder and make faces at the camera. However, what made me nervous was my dhoti, whose knots I felt were loosening with every step. Since I know that Lord Krishna would not come to my

aid and cover me with an infinite length of dhoti should fate
disrobe me, I moved very slowly taking care of my steps. And
with electric wires and camera power chords running around
everywhere I was doing exactly the right thing.

I cannot emphasize how dangerous videocameras at
weddings are. For everyone. First of all the cameramen make
you look stupid. They will stand and record you *while* you
are posing for the still photographers. The problem with this
is not immediately apparent. You will realize it later when
you watch the video with other people. Then you will feel
embarrassed as you see yourself first smiling for the camera,
then suddenly wiping that artificial smile off the face and
grumbling to the person next to you and then suddenly smiling
again in an exaggerated fashion – with the whole sequence
caught on tape.

That's not all. The videocamera captures stuff you thought
no one noticed. For instance, when I was a kid I remember
enormous merriment and mirth in family circles over a marriage
video where the wife, bedecked in her bridal finery, was
captured on camera counting the currency notes she had got
as gift and putting it surreptitiously into a purse. Don't think
that just because you are a guest, these videographer buggers
will save you from embarrassment. No no. They get perverted
pleasure in capturing you in fragranti delicto – when water is
running from your nose while biting into a spicy chilli chicken
piece, when you are burping after a heavy meal, when you are
spitting out a stubborn bit of bone onto the plate and when you
are double-dipping at the buffet line. This is why I do not trust
the video-men during weddings and I urge you not to either.

Presently, I was escorted by my wife's uncles to the groom's
seating area and asked to sit on an ornate throne. I felt like

a king. No, not really. Actually, I felt like a fool with the cameramen making me move my face to every angle and capturing me in what I later realized were the most unflattering of angles, so I looked even fatter than I was. If the persistent cries of 'Light up this side…no…no not that side… from the top' were not disorienting enough, strange people (whom I had never seen before and am unlikely to ever see again) were coming and introducing themselves to me.

To be honest, everyone looked the same. I smiled stupidly at the ceaseless procession of relatives and muttered something inane like, 'Oh I have heard so much about you.' Of course I never had.

For instance, this was the first time I got to know that my wife had so many sisters and lady friends.

I could not look at them too closely for the sake of decency, of course. No one likes it if the groom is ogling at other girls, specially the saalis. In order to exercise self-control and bring to my gaze an appropriate sense of disinterested calmness, I convinced myself these girls were actually guys. This invariably works for me.

Perhaps they thought I was being rude. Could not be helped. Better than to be considered a lech. One thing I could not help noticing, even amidst my carefully cultivated aloofness, was that my wife's sisters' ages had a wide distribution. As a friend of mine told me: That's a good investment for the future. You get my drift, right?

Soon it was time for the first phase of the wedding. That is the 'ashirbaad', or blessing. It is when the bride's family blesses the groom and the groom's family blesses the bride with the ceremonies happening almost concurrently in two different rooms. The way this works is that the guy who is blessing (the blessor) touches the blessee's head with some grass (not the 'mind-blowing mahiya' type but the one that grows from the ground and which cows eat), while you touch their feet in a gesture of obeisance.

Very empowering, is it not?

But the good thing is that the act of touching feet brings in many gifts as its happy consequence. This is a big thing for the groom, if he be as big a gift-slut as me.

At this time, allow me to vent a bit. Why oh why do people seem to think it's fine to buy gifts for the bride but not for the groom?

Hello!

In case you have not noticed, there is another person getting married too! I mean, if women are equal to men, why not have the same principle be carried over with regard to the disbursement of gifts? Why the sexism here, eh?

This social injustice had been an issue that had bothered me ever since I saw my uncle getting married when I was ten years old. I noticed that he hardly got anything in comparison to what my aunt did.

I have been told that a mature married man is expected to feel genuinely happy that people get presents for his wife and not for him. After all, as a loving partner one should feel joy that the person you adore is contented and be able to rise above petty selfishness. Yes, I do understand that. But I feel it is sad that my spouse is consistently deprived of this deliriously beautiful 'reflected pleasure'.

(Incidentally, to my in-laws reading this, I am very happy with the gifts I got. No, I am not an ungrateful bastard. Well, not too much anyways.)

But try as I could, I could just not get my mind off the gifts. Smiling and touching feet on the outside, my 'fearing the worst' brain was racing: 'What gift is Sulolita Aunty getting me? Hope not the same stuff we gave her when she got married fifteen years ago' and 'When my daughter gets married I will make sure to open the gifts then and there and on the basis of perceived value, route people into three buffet lines: premium (two non-veg items), normal (one non-veg item) and free (as much water and love as one can give).'

Distracted by such exalted thoughts, I forgot to notice that my shoes had been stolen.

Now during this ashirbaad ceremony you have to take off your shoes. Just like in any other Hindu religious ceremony, wearing shoes during a holy ceremony is not the done deal. Unfortunately, no doubt influenced by *Hum Aapke Hain Kaun*, one of the most culturally significant Hindi movies ever, people have revived this age-old irritating tradition of stealing the groom's shoes with gusto. The tradition is that the groom is supposed to be teased and then asked to pay the wife's cousins to get his shoes back.

In times when the grooms were milking the brides dry with their dowry demands, perhaps there was some poetic justice in turning the tables. Now it makes no sense. But then again, I would not be doing a traditional marriage if I skipped these traditions. My only belief is that this is not even a Bengali tradition but inspired by Punjabi weddings and inserted into tradition by a Hindi movie.

Not that this stealing of shoes is not fun. It is immensely joyous when there are lots of young people on both sides of the family and the ice needs to be broken between the nubile nymphets and eager dudes on either side with a 'Joote de do paise le lo' song. However, in my case, there was not anyone young from my side, no Salman Khan-type character who would vigorously shake his pelvis and swing from the chandelier while hitting the 'kudiyans' with the proverbial 'danas'. (Most people from my side had spondilitis.) Hence the shoe stealing was a damp squib.

Even then the shoes are supposed to be stolen when the wedding is in progress, not before it has even started. The people who stole the shoes (little kids, really) during the ashirbaad did not know better and sort of jumped the gun. For this, they were suitably chastised and asked to return the shoes. Of course, the impression that my would-be in-laws possibly got from my morose, slightly irritated face was that I am a mean-minded ogre who did not like to be made fun of.

Which really is not far off the mark.

But that was not the way I wanted to present myself on this very special day of my life. The shoe episode left the younger generation of my in-laws sullen and perhaps a bit more in awe/fear/loathing of me than I deserved.

After the ashirbaad was concluded, the actual wedding was to start. It was time. I was now supposed to change into the clothes provided by the bride's side. Here again, in deference to my wishes for personal space, I was taken to a room next to the kitchen that was being used as a storeroom. There the barber from the bride's side changed my dhoti.

In case people are shocked, I should remind them I did keep my underwear on during this change of clothes, though theoretically you are not supposed to even have a 'stitch' on your body during the ceremony. (The dhoti and the thin cloth covering your body do not have any stitches on them.) Fat chance of me going stichless though. The idiot who came up with this idea must have had a severe case of jock-itch himself. Ewwwww!

In the opening act of the Bengali wedding ceremony, the groom stands and the wife comes up to him, accompanied by her relatives, with a leaf covering her face. This is done to pay lip service to the tradition that the groom and the bride are supposed to be meeting for the first time in the wedding hall. This 'seeing for the first time' is known as shubho-drishti, which could roughly be translated as 'pleasing vision'.

Though I am sure when people actually did see each other for the first time seconds before getting married, it might not have been a pleasing experience for most of them – what with the number of times the bride must have taken the leaf off and seen an old sod, less the man of her dreams and more Tutankhamen's mummy, standing there with a toothless grin on his face. Or the groom coming face to face with a totally different woman than the one he understood he was going to marry (bride-switching being a not unheard-of practice).

Before the bride brings down the leaf covering her face, she has to circle the groom seven times. Which, considering my girth, must have been like walking around the outside track of an athletics field! It seems only in Brahmin (high-caste) weddings are the bride and the groom both supposed to go around the fire (which is how we think all Hindu marriages take place). Alas not for us low-caste people.

According to custom, however, the bride is not supposed to walk but is to be carried on a 'pinri' (a small wooden stool) to the ceremony. What I mean by 'carried' is that she is to be held aloft in the air by her brothers and other men in the family, then made to do her rounds and exchange garlands thus suspended. I think the origin of this tradition was in those pre-Rammohan Roy days when girls as young as ten would be married. Then, for obvious reasons, it would be convenient to physically lift and carry them to the marriage venue to prevent them from running away.

Without casting aspersions on my would-be wife's weight, I would say that it would have needed quite a few mustandas (muscled men) to hold her aloft and carry her around seven times. Since nobody on her side had good health insurance coverage, this tradition was dispensed with. Actually, in some places, even the groom is lifted in the air and there is a competition as to who is lifted higher – the groom or the bride. Since holding me up would even make even Atlas 'shrug' and say, 'I may lift the world on my shoulders. But arre yaar, main bhi insaan hoon,' I also stayed on the ground.

So the bride did the 1600-m walk unassisted and stopped in front of me. She then took away the leaf that covered her face and looked into the abyss that would be her future. At the same time, for some strange reason I have not been able to fathom, a white cloth was held aloft over the groom and bride's heads while the ladies of the house moved their tongues inside their mouths from which emanated a strange devilish cadence that sounded like 'Loo loo loo'.

Does that sound hilarious?

It is.

We then exchanged garlands. Thrice for the wedding and several times for each person who had a camera! To make the confusion even more confounded, people keep on shouting their opinions as to the 'right' way to exchange garlands – through each other's hands, elbows straight or crossed, head bent or up.

Of course the barber is present there to add his unique touch to the proceedings. According to tradition, this is the part of the whole evening when the two barbers are supposed to fight each other with rhyme. But since my iconoclast dad did not have a high idea of barber-bards and had not drafted one along (as previously mentioned), the barber from my wife's side stood unchallenged.

And he took advantage of this unipolar world, like George Bush, to unleash some serious pain in the form of a rap-like rhyme which had, among other things, references to women in their second marriages and to those having their periods.

Why? Again I have no idea.

This poetry was supposed to be funny and I knew it was not. The people who were laughing were doing it out of courtesy and to relax their jaws sore from the 'Loo loo loo' cries (technically called 'ullu'-ing). How did I know the laughter was artificial? It was exactly the same kind of merriment people exhibit when I crack a joke or pass a supposedly witty comment.

Then the ceremony, the Vedic one, started in front of the fire. The bride and I sat down cross-legged on the ground on small two-inch-high stools, i.e. the same pinris used before. Even there I could not sit normally. One of the priests told me to sit in such a manner that only the extremity of my toe touched the ground but not the rest of me, a Bolshoi ballet-like feat that I endeavoured to attempt. Keeping that pose, I was worried that my dhoti, which had started moving up my thighs, was revealing more skin than was appropriate.

My principal concern, however, was to keep myself from breaking out into peals of laughter. The reason for that was the venerable priest. Perhaps because he was not confident of his Sanskrit or maybe because he was just the shy sort, but the man kept muttering the mantras to himself. Was he invoking the gods? Or was he uttering imprecations under his breath, perhaps pissed off at his 'pronami' (remuneration)?

What I did know was that during each incantation to my ancestors he was getting my grandfather's, my father's and even my name wrong. Every time my name became something different – Anirban, Archisman, etc., and yes, he got even my wife's name wrong.

So, as far as the registrar who sits up in the heaven is concerned, who goes only by what he hears from the mouth of a Brahmin, someone else's son got married to some other lady.

No loss.

What, however, could have been a personal loss would have been the flaming objects that threatened to pop out of the fire. For some reason, I had to chuck bananas into the fire and, once inside, the bananas seemed to acquire a life of their own, crackling and moving. I was petrified one flaming shard would fly out, my dhoti would catch fire and the videographers would have one marvellous 'Man on Fire' Youtube moment.

Presently, before that could happen, the priest tied the knot. This means tying the thin fabric that covered my torso to my wife's sari, making me now officially a bull tethered to the pole.

This was followed by the weird stunt wherein you are supposed to put shindoor (vermillion) on your wife's forehead with a blunt earthen instrument that looks more like a hand grenade than something to apply shindoor with. The catch is you are not allowed to look at your wife as you do it. While taking this shot in the dark you are supposed to, at the same time, pull a cloth over her head signifying that from now on you take responsibility of her.

Finally, you stand up, hold your wife from the back and both of you pour flattened rice into the fire. Don't ask me why, it's all in the book.

All the rituals were finished by 10 at night. There were photo-ops galore after that, standing with every subset of relatives you could think of.

It was then that I realized I was damn hungry. For food, that is.

My dad told me that during your own wedding, food should be the last thing on your mind.

For me that was hardly so.

I normally never sit in the last batch of a wedding. It's the time when there is more gravy then pieces of meat, the pieces of fish are the broken ones, the servers have apologetic grins on their faces and the predominant sound you hear when you ask for second servings is the unmistakable clang of a spoon scraping the bottom of the pot. Now that the wedding was over, I was coming to understand that my place in the sun was also a thing of the past, like an old film star whose autograph no one cares for.

After the guests have left, there is the Bengali tradition in which people are supposed to not let the newly-weds sleep. The younger generation of in-laws, no doubt licking their wounds after the shoe incident earlier in the evening, dozed off to sleep without bothering me. My wife's friends asked me to sing. But there was not much cajoling, and needless to say I was not going to exercise my nightingale-like voice unless my ego was massively stroked.

After all, Kumar Sanu does not perform if you just ask him once.

Well just as I thought I was going to heed their non-insistent requests, they fell asleep. And I did not want to wake them up as well as the others. It was a nice opportunity for both of us to catch some sleep. After all, my poor wife had been suffering even more than me because the rituals for the bride are more elaborate. Now was the best time for us to sleep. There was a minor technicality however. Everybody was asleep and there was no bedding for us.

Ultimately, late late at night we did get a place to rest our heads. The story stops here. The rest is left to the imagination.

To be honest, it was not over yet, there would be some ceremonies the next day, and copious weeping during the vidaai (farewell). My younger in-laws had such a bad impression of me they did not even ask me for the money they are supposed to get for keeping the groom up all night, which in any case they did not. So I had to search them out and give them the money, so that they would have fond memories of their jijaji, at least on the day he got married. This was followed the day after by the groom's reception where I wore a shoe two sizes too small, a person came to the wrong reception and took back the gift he handed me, and the fruit salad ran out by the time I came to the table – well, a long story!

What any shrink will tell you is that the important thing about life experiences is what insights about the world and about yourself you are able to carry forward.

My first realization was that an Indian marriage ceremony is intentionally kept lengthy and torturous so that no one in their right mind would ever want to get married twice. That's the problem with Western marriages: they are too short and painless. Hence the high divorce rate in the US and Europe. Over here we have perfected a marriage technique such that the groom is repeatedly reminded of his responsibilities through the chanting of the same mantras over and over again. He is made to sit in revealing clothing so that people can see he is more or less in decent physical shape. His suppleness is tested by the ballerina toes. His intuition is tested by his putting the vermillion without looking at the bride. How easily he can part with cash is gauged by how graciously he is able to tip all and sundry. Finally, his even temper is tested by his ability to keep a good-humoured smile on his face throughout the whole process.

Among the other insights I gleaned from this experience was how ephemeral fame is and how you should cherish every second of it. No matter how much I disliked being the centre of attraction, it felt a whole lot worse when everything was over and I went back to being my regular Joe once again.

Most importantly, that day did change me in a very significant way. It was that day which made me the most important person in my wife's life. Hopefully forever. That's what made it worth the while. No matter how insignificant I may be, no matter how many regret letters I receive from prospective employers and 'you goofed up again' letters from my boss, no matter how fat I may become, there is one person to whom I will always be number one. Once the music dies, the glitter of ornaments vanish into the night, the flowers wither away and the months become years, that is the only feeling that remains.

CHAPTER 10

Your Guide to Making a Fortune in Television

This is it, people – the document that the Ektaa Kapoors of the world do not want you to read. If you have always wanted to gain fame, fortune and immortality by scripting winning Hindi sitcoms, soap operas, reality shows (yes reality shows too need a bit of scripting) and commercially viable news (yes yes, this too can be written) but never quite knew how to go about it, well, now the wait is over.

SECTION 1: HINDI SOAPS

But before I reveal the ancient secrets of writing Hindi soaps to you, first I need to know whether you are worthy.

Here is the first test. Take a long hard look at the man in the mirror. Are you a creative person who has original ideas? Do you think the medium of television should be used to create something of enduring artistic value? Do you define the word 'reality' as the 'untampered, un-manipulated truth'?

Were your favourite television comedies *Yeh Jo Hain Zindagi, Flop Show, Mungeri Lal Ke Haseen Sapne?* Do you define excellence in drama with *Buniyaad* or *Tamas?* Do you miss *Qile Ki Rahasya* and *Mirza Ghalib?*

If you answered 'yes' to any of these questions, writing a winning Hindi sitcom/reality show in today's entertainment environment is not for you. I am sorry for being so blunt but there is no other way for me to break the news. Better you look for an alternative career repairing old black and white television sets.

For the rest, no need to bring out the champagne yet. I have yet another question.

What is your name?

Write down that answer and read the next part only after you have completed the exercise.

If your answer was just your name, then consider yourself disqualified.

If your answer was 'My name is –' then all I can say is that you have an aptitude for writing complete answers.

And oh, you also are disqualified.

For those of you who filled up a whole foolscap sheet of paper before arriving at the answer (i.e. your name), you have potential. You may want to hang around.

Finally, for those of you who filled up full ten sheets and yet did not once say what your name was, you are exactly the kind of person who will succeed in this field.

Brevity is the soul of wit. Sure.

But in the world of Hindi soaps, it is the definite 'serial killer'.

The reason for that is simple. Serials have to contain twenty-three minutes of material for a thirty-minute slot, with the intervening seven minutes being taken by advertisements. More precisely, they have to contain twenty-three minutes of 'filler' for the seven minutes of advertisement, which is the only seven minutes the channel and the producers care for.

Successful sitcoms/soaps have four new episodes per week (there was a time when they had one), and so every week you as a writer are obliged to belch out at least one hundred and twenty minutes of story. A sitcom/soap lasts for many months and the successful ones for years.

So unless you have Ved Vyas or some other similarly divine entity breathlessly dictating to you, it is unlikely you will be able to come up with an epic story which will remain engaging, original and fast-paced over 400 episodes.

And here is the most important thing.

Even if you, by some happy accident, do come up with such a masterpiece, no sponsor would want to touch it with a ten-foot pole.

They will instead guffaw in your face and say, 'Abbe, khud ko Krzysztof Kieslowski samajhta hai......arre sahib, hamen arty cheez thodi banane hain, hamen sirf detergent ke ads dikhaane hain.' Then they will throw the script in your face while laughing 'Ha ha ha ha', a laughter that will, in the best tradition of the Hindi sitcom, resonate for three minutes and kill precious one hundred and eighty seconds before another advertisement is sprung.

To be honest, they do have a point.

First understand that the typical audience for a Hindi soap is neither looking for intellectual stimulation nor are they much interested in a nuanced narrative with complicated, intersecting story arcs.

If they were, they would be reading a good book.

But they are not. In other words, they have made a choice, a choice you should respect.

Plus you also have to take into account the fact that your average audience member is not sitting at one place watching the sitcom. She is not wrapped in that state of total absorption that one is in a dark movie theatre or in bed when curled up with a book.

No.

She is talking to someone on the phone, packing lunch for her daughter, boxing the ear of her naughty son who has not done his homework, adjusting the gas burner after the pressure cooker has sounded the whistle, haggling with the vegetable seller, and at the same time watching television.

Maintaining such extreme levels of multitasking that would challenge even a quad core processor, how can you expect anyone, even a Marie Curie, to follow a complicated and more importantly a fast-paced story?

Imagine you have a serial where the plot moves fast. Now consider typical viewer, Shefali Aunty, forty-five years old with three kids. It's 2 o'clock in the afternoon. She is sinking into her sofa, the layers of fat from her waist jiggling in a tired rhythm after a morning of work – seeing the kids off to school and catching up on the latest gossip about the promiscuous divorcee on the upper floor.

She turns on the TV. Her favourite soap is on.

A few minutes later, the bell rings. She opens it. It is Simran, the newly married girl who has moved into the next floor. She asks Shefali Aunty if she has any sugar for she needs to make some tea. Shefali Aunty looks out at the landing. A rather handsome man is standing there. This is not her husband.

Simran, by way of explaining says, 'This is Ravi. He is a distant cousin...'

Shefali Aunty cannot restrain a knowing smile. Yes, a handsome 'cousin' who happens to show up when husband is at work. It's not the first time she has seen the face in the apartment. A few days ago, he was standing near the sweet shop to protect himself from the rains. And a few days before that, she had again seen him in the afternoon waiting near the bus stand.

Yes, she would not forget that face.

She closes the door. And then she puts a call through to Pratibha Aunty. Her servant picks up the phone and says, 'Memsahab is taking a bath.' Shefali Aunty has to tell someone, else she will pop a nerve in her eye. So she calls Savitha Aunty and they discuss, in hushed whispers, about the rather diligent 'cousin' who visits the newly wed Simran. Today's girls… they agree!

After this satisfactory interlude, Shefali Aunty returns to the sofa, a full twenty minutes after she left it.

Her soap is still on.

Now if that serial had a fast-paced narrative with a plot that needed to be consistently 'followed' Shefali Aunty would be totally and absolutely lost.

What would she do then?

She would mutter to herself and just change the channel. And miss the advertisements that were coming in a few seconds. If the story was really dynamic, she would be lost even the next day when she tuned in. Soon she would lose interest forever and just shift her loyalty to a competing soap.

A pair of eyeballs would be irretrievably lost.

This the powers-that-be just cannot allow.

Consequently, they want a very slow, almost static narrative that flows like a stream of mercury. Such that when Shefali

Aunty sits back on her sofa or Pratibha Aunty comes out of the bathroom wiping her hair, the story would be exactly at the same spot where she left it and she can continue without having to connect any kind of dots.

Remember the following if you forget everything else:

THE AUDIENCE DOES NOT WANT TO THINK

Highlight that with a marker. Burn it onto your chest, *Ghajini*-style.

If you make them think, make one even neuron spark, then the game is up. The channel is changed before you can say 'Saas and Bahu'.

Another thing. In order to keep brain activity to a minimum, every character in the story must be unquestionably black or undisputedly white. Realistic characters with shades of grey who behave like real people are a strict no-no because the audience does not want to waste brain cycles deliberating on whether a certain character is good or bad.

They want quick and easy answers. It is your job as the scriptwriter to make the identification of characters and their motivations as simple as you possibly can. Remember, the moment the camera focuses on a character's face, its alignment to the dark or light side should be self-evident. Else the audience gets confused and detached.

So what about these dark and light character classes?

Insiders refer to them as the Alok Nath and the Duryodhana stereotype.

1. The Alok Nath–Nirupa Roy stereotype: These people are so full of the milk of human kindness that foamy froth

bubbles out from every pore. They are ready to sacrifice body organs for the neighbour's son, always keep their hands folded in a namaskar and even though their eyes are perennially wet like Cherrapunji in the monsoon, not an evil word ever escapes their lips.

When the camera focuses on them, they are immediately recognizable by their tremulous pity-inducing visages, or alternatively, their ever-present beatific smiles that even six-month-old babies would envy.

2. The Duryodhana–Manthara evil stereotype: These are those who make an old woman kneel down and rub her nose on the ground when she comes to ask for money for a life-saving operation for her blind and deaf daughter. These incarnations of evil discriminate against the girl child, double it if her complexion is dark (as an aside, a dark child is called Saonli and a fair child is named Sweta – again so that the audience does not have to think too much). They scheme, plot, murder, deprive widows of their property and commit every act of heartlessness known to man. And just when you think you have seen every act of cruelty you possibly could, they surprise you by forcing mothers to feed their babies with food that has been intentionally dropped on the floor.

Being evil of course has to show on their faces. This means that they are obliged to perennially snarl, roll their eyes and twist their lips. Even when they act sweet while laying a trap for the good, they have to periodically look at the camera and make evil expressions. This has to be done so that the audience has no doubt as to what their true intentions are.

By this time you have probably been convinced of the need to keep it simple and extremely slow. This brings us to the next question – how do you kill time and prolong a threadbare story?

Here below are some standard techniques.

SETTING THE CONTEXT

It should be plain as water to the most brain-dead of you that the principal intention of the narrator should be not to lose the audience. As a matter of fact, in the best traditions of the Hindi serial, I have said it quite a few times already in different ways.

At the start of every episode, set the context with an elaborate 'what happened last time'. Before each advertisement, show the audience what will happen after the advertisement, since people have a proclivity to reset their brain while watching endorsements for health drinks and packaged parathas. And at the very end of the episode…yes, you got it…spend another minute in showing what will happen next time.

The benefit is two-fold. Even those with the attention span of a two-month-old can follow the story if you keep repeating story elements. Most importantly, you waste TV time, time you, the scriptwriter, would otherwise have to fill up with your brain-droppings.

THE ROUND-ROBIN SHOTS

An extremely common trick, whose enduring popularity is a testament to its effectiveness, this technique is based on having a large number of characters all assembled in one scene.

Consider the following. The chocolate-face hero is getting married. His entire family (and Hindi serial families are like platoons) is assembled. Just as he is about to take the pheres, in comes a fetching woman and claims to be his wife.

Now this is where the trick is sprung. As the second woman comes in and says, 'Ruko, main iski biwi hoon,' (Stop I am his wife) the camera starts focusing on each person in the room (which may be as high as twenty). It zooms in and lingers on one person. On cue, an exaggerated expression registers on the focused face.

If you are a good person (like the old family servant) your face has an expression of shock and concern. If you, however, are a servant of evil, like the hero's aunt who wants to deprive the good people of their inheritance, you curl your lips up in an evil, knowing snarl, leaving no doubt to the most vegetated of your audience that you are behind this shocking interlude.

After thirty seconds have elapsed, the camera moves to another shocked visage. And then on to another till each of the twenty persons has had thirty seconds of camera time. (Note: Ten minutes have elapsed and nothing has happened.)

Once this round is over, you have 10 seconds of 'What will happen next'.

This sets the stage for the main part. Advertisements.

Messages from the sponsors are then followed by ten seconds of 'What happened before the break'.

Then the fun starts all over again.

The hero's mother says, 'Tum kaun ho, beti?' (Who are you, my daughter?)

Immediately the camera gets into action for another full round scan of the assembled party, eating up another ten minutes of episode time.

THE MUSICAL INTERLUDE

Long a staple of Bollywood, used principally to stretch the plot and fly the characters to exotic foreign locales, the song is a vital arrow in the quiver of anyone writing a mega-serial. Unlike movie producers, you are not expected to spend a lot of money on these songs. Hell, you are not even expected to create anything new. Just copy a hit song from a movie and make the hero-heroine dance to it. Six minutes can effortlessly be eaten up in this exercise and it also allows the actors, typically Bollywood rejects, to indulge in a few 'what could have been' moments.

THE PICNIC

This technique refers to the device of throwing in an arbitrary event that has nothing to do with the main thread of the plot. This may be a family picnic, a cricket match, a birthday party or a visit to a temple. Ostensibly done for character development, they do to an episode or two what cigarettes do to the lungs.

SIDE PLOTS AND EXTRANEOUS CHARACTERS

If in the unlikely event you are running out of ideas as to how to prolong the story, the simplest thing is to bring in new characters and outlandish story extensions. Remember nothing is too bizarre in the world of Hindi soaps – after all, this is the only place where it is literally true that the child is the father of man, with the character who plays the mother often looking younger than the one playing the daughter.

In this fantastic world, not an eyebrow will be raised if

1) In the seventieth episode you bring in a long-lost sister of the hero – an ichchhadari nagin whose life has been pawned to an evil tantrik.

Or

2) In the fifty-third episode, the newly wed belle is possessed by the ghost of the husband's first wife.

Or

3) In the 300th episode, the lady who was killed off with a bullet to her brain in the 113th episode comes back as an amnesiac who however remembers to take revenge on her killers.

Or

4) A pair of coochie-coo lovers realize that they were husband-wife in their previous life and had been murdered by the same evil person who is trying to kill them off in this life, a person who is so evil that his looks have not changed through the generations (except a streak of grey).

THE SLAP

Secret market research has shown that one thing the Indian audience cannot resist is the slap.

As the legendary Dang from *Karma* said:

'Dang ko yeh thappad ka goonj hamesha yaad rahega.'

Any serial that wishes to strike it big has to have a number of slaps. Slaps also have another benefit – they are excellent footage-eaters.

This is the way the whole thing works. First, the tension is built up through many iterations of the round-robin shot technique with two protagonists snarling at each other.

Then the slap lands like a Sachin Tendulkar punch through cover-point, with the centre of percussion making a sweet sound.

The screen goes from colour to black and white in a flash. Back to colour.

And then the slap is action-replayed as if this is a run-out waiting for a third-umpire decision. The sound of palm hitting cheek is made to echo.

Again the screen transits from colour to black and white and back again.

Then the camera swings once again into the round-robin mode, catching each expression from the long-suffering old mother's teary eyes to the evilly enjoying expression of the caretaker's son whose lecherous advances had been rejected by the slapped girl in the fourteenth episode.

Wait, we are not done. The slap is action-replayed again – this time from a different angle. And yes, the camera goes into a second round of circulation.

Yes. One whole episode is taken up by one slap. That is how brilliantly useful these instruments of domestic violence are. And remember this moment can again be milked in the future as part of flashbacks to be used to remind viewers the reason they should not feel sorry for the slapper when she is struck by lightning on a stormy day in the 211th episode.

Finally, in passing, a few words on the other common conventions of the Hindi soap which you should follow if you want to be successful in this field.

1. Sets have to be marvellously extravagant, assaulting the senses with a riot of colours. People do not live in houses. They live in furniture stores. Remember that subtlety and realism are your enemies when it comes to set design.

2. Women always have to wear gaudy jewellery. Even while being forced to steal half a scrap of dry bread to feed your infant, you should never consider the possibility of selling the Rs 50 lakh worth of gold that adorns your body.

3. In the same spirit of opulent 'Behenji shining', women always have to be dolled up in the gaudiest of saris and be as made-up as if they are going to or coming back from a wedding. Yes, always. Even when they have just got up from bed, even when they are dying in a hospital, and even when they are in jail.

Even though Hindi serials have a happy habit of dragging on following the principle 'Love is all about never having to say goodbye', I shall desist from doing so and move onto the next topic.

SECTION 2: REALITY SHOWS

Reality shows, like the 'India ki Phatee Bansoori', 'Kaun Banegi Garbhavati' and the 'Naach Basanti Naach', belong to a genre that has of late become the hottest commodity in the Indian television market.

First principles first. Reality is boring. It consists of standing in line, being crowded in like sardines on the 8 o'clock local, of being screwed by the system and of finding that good guys finish last.

Reality shows, however, are different. Wise men would interpret them as our stance against the inevitability of destiny, an affirmation of our ability as human beings to manipulate what we have been told is the preserve of the gods.

Manipulate. That is the magic word.

No no, I do not mean manipulate the results or somehow contrive to have popular contestants to be not voted out. Oh no, that would be the most unethical thing to do. That I have been told, on good authority, never happens. Just like matches never get fixed in cricket.

When I use the word 'manipulate' I mean manipulate the audience. Manufacture the drama. Milk audience sympathy. Get them involved with the fate of the contestants.

For instance, in singing talent competitions, whenever a candidate comes on stage, it is obligatory to show their parents and brother and their so-sweet family moments. It is even more important to highlight their personal struggles, with all kinds of sentimental sad music in the background.

Now, some people may ask what the fact that the pet dog Bhulu of contestant number 8 died recently or that his third-removed aunt had a knee-replacement operation, tragic as these are, has to do with the ability of the contestant to hit the high notes. Ergo, why does it need so much airtime?

The reason is that reality shows are judged as successful, like everything else in the television world, by the eyeballs it gets and the advertising revenue it generates. For that to happen, people need underdog stories. They need this so that they may empathize, continue to tune in and then spend the requisite amount to send a text message to vote.

In any case, the contestants are universally so talented that the general public has no other means to distinguish between Payal from Mumbai and Somchandra from Kolkata than to fall back on the contestant that they 'like' the most.

So what guides this liking for a particular contestant over the other? There is, of course, empathy and sympathy as previously discussed.

An even more important contributory factor to this 'liking' is community and regional pride. Balaishankar Ray or Sanjay Phadkar aren't just individuals with great voices. Even more importantly, they are representatives of the cities and the communities to which they belong. As a scriptwriter of a reality show, it is one of your primary responsibilities to cement the association of individuals with their city or language so that people take time out from their lives to cheer for the 'local' boy or girl. This is to be done by continually making the judges and the anchors refer to them as 'Bangal ka tiger' or as 'Maharashtra ki shaan' or 'Delhi ka Dulara'.

Remember that without this association no one will much care for Balaishankar Ray. After all how many of us stop to help a stranger lying on a road bleeding from his head even if we know he speaks the same language as we do. Not that we are heartless or selfish but it's just that we do not have the time to get involved.

But market the same man as 'Bangal ka tiger' and he immediately becomes one of us. Magically, we now have the time as well as the money to get involved, run fan clubs, greet him at the airport with garlands and keep text voting till our balances run out. Should he win, we bask in the reflected glory of the tiger's achievement till, of course, the next reality show star that represents 'us' comes along, at which point of time Balaishankar Ray goes back to being a man on the street.

Of course, as a show writer you have to realize that not all people who tune into reality programmes do so just to enjoy the cornucopia of talent on offer or to revel in the good fortune of others. Many people just want to enjoy the spectacle – the public humiliation of contestants and the fights between the judges. Just like the many people who watch Formula 1 racing just for the crashes and the wrecks.

A year and a few months ago, the UK and of course India went into a tizzy about racist remarks against our very own Shilpa Shetty on a reality show called *Big Brother*. The point that most people forgot to stress upon, amidst all the outrage and the displays of patriotism, was that racism in this context was not so much an expression of a nation's inherent insensitivity towards minorities but an instrument used by one contestant to mentally harass another contestant on a reality show. If Shilpa Shetty hadn't been brown, she would have been harassed based on her sexual orientation, her weight, her looks or her intelligence – but since she could not be pulled down on the first three, and the other contestants didn't have much to show in terms of brain matter, the only thing that they had left was her skin colour.

Reality shows are a lot about humiliation and conflict. After all, what's more entertaining than to see people fight and subject themselves to abject humiliation for the sake of money? As the great Bullah from *Gunda* said:

'Maza aata hai. Jab insaan paison ke liye kutton ki tarah ladta hain. To mujhe bahoot maza aata haiiii...'

(I get great joy when people fight like dogs for money. I get great joyyyyyyyy...)

This spectacle of public conflict makes us feel thankful that at least when we fight at office meetings or get chewed out by the boss for losing a contract, the whole nation is not a witness to our shame. And perhaps it is that sense of 'feeling superior' that enables us to enjoy the seamy side of reality shows.

Whatever be the socio-psychological reasons for this morbid fascination with 'real conflict', as a writer you are obliged to script some of the things that people want. Again, I am not saying that you should give judges prepared scripts to regulate their spontaneous reactions. But when two judges get up and start exchanging barely concealed barbs at each other with words like 'With due respect' and 'Main aap ka kadar karta hoon magar...' your role should be to catch the friendly interaction with multiple camera angles and later present it with selective editing so as to make things more 'dramatic' than it actually was. If this somewhat pricks your conscience let me say that this should not be construed as an advice to manufacture reality but simply as an exhortation to package truth in an attractive way.

As a reality show creator what you really hope for (not that, of course, you can create such situations yourself for that would definitely BE as unethical as admiring another woman despite being married) is that you get the right kind of contestants (vile, aggressive, bitchy and sometimes with a few screws loose) and the right kind of judges (caustic, opinionated and rude). Once you do that, you only need to throw them together in the ring, add one spark here and another there, sit back and then enjoy the 'spontaneous' combustion on national TV.

There. That's your job. To add the spark that starts the fire. If you have two lissome lasses fighting for the attention of one cool dude, your job is to, off camera of course, stroke the burning embers. And then when the tongues of the flame come out, you have to capture the cat-fight in all its pristine glory.

If you have a judge with a caustic, acerbic tongue, you should encourage him to be as nasty as possible. And if luck be good, and a pathetic performer with an exaggerated idea of her capabilities comes face to face with such an honestly brutal judge, sit back and enjoy the thrust and counter-thrust. Just do not forget to keep recording. And never, never rush in with the first- aid package. Let there be blood on the floor. You can always mop it up after the cameras have stopped rolling.

SECTION 3: NEWS AND CURRENT AFFAIRS

If you thought reality shows could not be scripted, prepare for the next shock. News has also to be scripted and packaged. After all, remember that in today's world of cable channels news has to compete for viewership with soaps and reality shows and thus have to be similarly engaging and addictive.

Yes yes, I know. There are some stiff-necked people who still do not get it. From some misplaced sense of propriety stemming from a belief that the news is the holiest of holies and should be presented without any masala, they pine for those colourless days of Doordarshan when robotic anchors would barf out a 'what ribbons did they cut today' log of the activities of mighty ministers. Since we did not have a choice in those days we had to grin and bear it, just like we had to tolerate live coverage of the SAARC (South Asian Association for Regional Cooperation) summit.

But now we do have a choice. And we choose to exercise it.

The big question that you need to answer is: What IS news?

The wrong way to approach the solution would be to follow the advice of the stiff-necked people. That is, to identify the most important things that happened today with the importance being defined as 'historical significance', 'potential for affecting society' and 'critical for public awareness' and present them in a neutral, balanced fashion.

If you go down this path, you would consider farmer suicides, policy and planning, lack of border security and similar other 'boring' stuff to be what the headlines should be made of.

But then again, that's the wrong old Boy Scout way of thinking.

The right way to go about things is, instead, to ask the question, 'What do people want to see?' After all in a democracy, that's all that counts.

Do you think people want to hear	
This?	Or this?
Public health crisis in a remote corner of the country	Amitabh Bachchan catching a cold
An exposé on the declining state of urban infrastructure	How a starlet's puppy dog saved her from being stuck in the Mumbai rains
Farmer suicides in Vidharbha	Who will dance at the greatest event in history after the Asvamedha Yagna of the Pandavas – the Abhi–Ash wedding?
The result of a study on the state of primary education in rural India	The result of a study on the bedroom habits of Indian urban couples
The murder of a poor unprivileged girl in a remote corner of India	The murder of an urban 'just like us' girl in a major metropolis
A current affairs programme	A programme about the 'current affairs' of celebrities – who got dumped and who is seeing whom

Besides the content, of course, there is the question of presentation. No one cares for the emotionless monotone newsreader voice reminiscent of the famous Khabarilal of *Tiranga*. Instead, they want to see some emotion and 'deramaa'...

Drama. Lots of it. Breaking news. Brought to you live. Fresh. Like garam samosa. Come madam, my jalebis are fresher than that channel at the corner.Ceaselessly mobile news ticker at the bottom. Shrill and dynamic newsmen and women moving through the burning city like superheroes. Thrusting mikes in the faces of the high and mighty. Grilling personalities and making hidden tapes. Shouting, haranguing and cutting in. There is gunfire. People screaming. Dramatic background music playing. A blood-splattered graphic in the background. The audience sits glued to the screen. Can you please pass me the ketchup – this is too thrilling.

Is this the reporting of news? Or is this the creation of it? If you think it is the first, SMS 01 to 3456. If you think it is the second, SMS 02 to 3456. Not that it matters. Our mind is made up anyway.

CHAPTER 11

Bollywood, Bollywood Na Raha

'Are you, like, checking me out?' asks Sunehri (Aishwarya Rai) of a Spanish-looking Mr A (Hrithik Roshan).

Kareena Kapoor's name in *Kabhi Khushi Kabhi Gham* is Pooja but being oh so la la modern she prefers people call her 'Poo', trying to be 'with-it' but perhaps unaware that poo typically means excreta ejected through the anal orifice.

In *Love Story 2050*, the hero tells the heroine hep-ly and ultra coolly: 'Tumhara life hai na, it's like hotdog without a sausage', the sexual imagery being unintentionally Freudian.

I confess. I just do not get the new internationalized wanna-be Bollywood, a world of burgers, fries, Coke, tank-tops and faux-accented American English. Just like I do not get SMS English and why people spell 'come' as 'cum' and then use it in sentences like, 'Why don't you and your misses cum together?'

Maybe I am too old-fashioned. Maybe I am too uncool. Maybe I yearn for those days in which tickets could be bought for Rs 20, when the pickpockets would jostle you at the entrance and not clear your pocket out legally at the soda-popcorn stand.

Call me a revisionist. Call me a romantic. But I really miss the old Bollywood of the '80s and the '90s. It is the comforting sameness that snobs nowadays call 'formulaic' and the jhinchaak innocence captured by the unspeakable magic of Mithun-da in tight silver trousers dancing to 'I am a disco dancer' that pumps up my desi heart in a way Hrithik or Harman can never do.

It's not as if the new wave of 'international' Bollywood is of an undisputedly higher standard. True, the technical quality is much improved over the golden '80s and '90s, and avant-garde directors use different types of lenses and filters, innovative camera angles, jump cuts, super slow motion and split screens. But for the most part (with very few exceptions) they are copies ('inspirations' being the politically correct term) of foreign flicks. The dumb/lazy guys lift Hollywood flicks scene-by-scene while the smart ones go for Korean, Malaysian, French and less mainstream celluloid creations that people are not likely to have seen.

In contrast, the Bollywood of the '80s and the '90s was definitely original.

Tell me, which other film industry could provide the surreal sight of ten men dressed in vampire costumes dancing lock-step with ten other men dressed as Chinese monks?[1]

Tell me, which country can give us cinematic poetry that blends the process of starting a car with the act of making love:

---

1 A sequence from the movie *Nakabandi* starring Dharmendra and Sridevi.

Pom pom pom pom
Yeh mamma mia mamma mia
Pyar ki gadi tez chalao (Drive the love car fast)
Accelerator (pronounced 'axilater') aur dabao (squeeze the accelerator hard.)[2]

Tell me, which director in the world has the imagination to conceive of a sequence where the hero (in white sweater, white trousers and white shoes) and the heroine (in a skimpy apsara sari) dance on the side of a green hill while an avalanche of a thousand lemons rolls down the slopes?[3]

But all that creativity is now a thing of the past. In its hurry to contemporanize itself, Bollywood has shed its defining skin – the endearing clichés, the wholesome characters and the simple linear predictable plots.

Working-class hero runs home with the trophy and falls at the feet of the long-suffering widowed mother with a gutsy 'Main college main first aaya hoon, maa (I have aced the college exam).' The mother looks at the picture of his deceased father saying, 'Aaj pitaji rahete to kitne khush hote (If your father were alive, he would be so happy),' and offers the son a plate of high-carb gajar ka halwa. On cue the darling sister enters and says, 'Abhi ek pyari si bhabhi laana padega, bhaiyya (Now you have to bring a sweet wife, brother).' Brother looks all shy. Mother says to the daughter, 'Kitni natkhat hai tu (How naughty hast thou become).'

Aah heaven.

---

2 The song from *Justice Chaudhury* starring Jeetendra and Sridevi.
3 This song you will find in the movie *Hoshiyaar* starring Jeetendra and Meenakshi Sheshadri.

Log jahaan par rahete hain (The place where people stay)
Us jagah ko log ghar kahete hain (They call it their home)
Hum is ghar main rahete hain (We stay in this house)
Isse pyar ka mandir kahete hain (We call it a temple of love)[4]

Not everything in old Bollywood was sunny and perfect, of course.

Cranky martinet (Shashikala or Bindu) would scream to the heroine: 'Kahaan se aayi hai mooh kala karke? (Where hast thou come from after darkening thy countenance?).' While she, full of old-world charm and sharam, would copiously weep in shame.

Now of course, in the new bolder Bollywood, before anyone can point fingers at her blackened face, the seductress proudly proclaims: 'Yeh jism pyar nahin jaanta hai, jaanta hai to sirf jism ki bhookh (This body does not know love, all it knows is the hunger for another body).'

To be honest, this boldness pisses me off. No, not because I am a silly sentimentalist with a fetish for Nirupa Roy. The dislike stems from a deep well of 'Where were these type of girls when I was growing up?' angst which people of my generation will surely understand.

If I could use one person as a metaphor for the metamorphosis of Bollywood, I need look no further than one of my favourites – David Dhawan. This is the man who gave us hours of rustic delirium that was quintessentially old school – big corpulent women raising their saris while Shakti Kapoor in a chaddi and baniyan crawled between their legs, rising up only to drop his

---

4 Movie: *Pyar Ka Mandir.*

chaddis to the tune of 'Aaa eee ooo uuuu', Govinda singing 'Ram narayan baja bajata' in sylvan surroundings and then executing the world-famous 'UP wala thumka' (subsequently adopted as the dance step of choice by millions of ordinary Indians).

Now that same Dhawan has abandoned his roots and gone 'international'. Sleek back-up dancers in stilettos have replaced the overweight 200-lb aunties, locales are now expensive and foreign, the hero dances hiphop Will Smith-style, wearing Eminem get-up, and sings Spanish: 'Marria Marria Senorita Marria tequiro tequiro.'

Which is a pity. Because in the middle of all the 'Love me love me say' and the 'aping' of the West, the old Dhawan and with him the Bollywood I loved is now buried for good. But at least 'we will always have Paris'[5], or more precisely, golden memories of lines like 'Teri naani mari to main kya karoon? (What the hell do I care if your grandma is dead?)' to keep us warm in the nuclear winter of *Shano Shano*.

As depressing as this transformation has been, what is even more painful is having to sit through Hindi copies of *The Exorcist, The Ring, The Grudge, What Lies Beneath* and assorted other foreign horror movies, with their slick special effects.and big budgets a weak substitute for the joyous energy and bountiful feel-good of the old Hindi horror classics (generically referred to as Ramsay movies after the brothers who made a number of such classics in the '80s and '90s).

And what was the general structure of these horrible horror flicks?

A gang of young college kids (average age of the actors somewhere in the forties) go for a pleasure trip to an ancient

---

5 The ultimate romantic line of *Casablanca*

dwelling (haveli) in the village, the kind of house where an ominous tune plays in the background and where the old chowkidar, perennially wrapped in a black shawl, always carries a lantern even though the sun is shining.

A crazy tantrik warns the kids about the murderous entity that haunts the house.

The rationalist westernized college boys and girls, raised perhaps on a diet of Marx and Richard Dawkins, of course do not heed the advice. If they did, there would be no film.

The monster presently manifests itself.

This devilish entity could be something as simple as a disembodied hairy hand with the habit of bursting out of dark corners when you most expect it, or something as nuanced as a man wearing an ill-fitting latex mask with red lights in his eyes. Its malignancy is explained by a back story which mandatorily consists of any three of the following: zamindars, nautch girls, multiple queens, sadhus, snakes and ancient curses.

The first corpse to hit the ground would be that of the nondescript friend of the heroine, the one with five words of dialogue and five seconds of screen time. She is followed on the path to hell by the overconfident city boy who had earlier made fun of the 'backward' villagers and their silly superstitions. The third to meet the maker is the voluptuous siren with a predilection for bathing fully clothed.

Thus, after the splattering of much tomato ketchup 'blood', the only ones left alive would be the noble-hearted hero, his virginal girlfriend and another young couple. Belying their instinct for self-preservation, they would then wander out alone at night into shadowy corners of the haveli, doing exactly the same things that had got their horror-movie predecessors into a lot of trouble. While all that you as an audience could do was to pray. Pray, so as to keep your heart from leaping out of your mouth as heads flew off like hot popcorn, blood-curdling screams echoed through the night and a looming presence manifested itself in each scene, which if you looked closely you realized were actually shadows of the unit members.

Alas, today these simple pleasures are gone. Buried like the vampire-werewolf-haiwaan with a stake through his heart. In its place, there are special-effects-laden derivative adaptations of horror movies from all over the world, lacking the most essential thing of a good horror yarn: a heart.

Just like the Ramsay genre, another thing that has become extinct, like the dodo birds, are those magicians who wore the most outlandish of costumes, sprouted the awesomest of lines, held hostage the hero's mother, made the heroine dance in his lair, and who overall seemed so intent on entertaining the audience that you wondered how they ever got any time to be evil.

Yes, I am talking about those men and women who made the hero look good: the villains.

Gabbar Singh of *Sholay*, the man whose name would make babies stop crying.

Mogambo of *Mr India*, whose state of bliss ('Mogambo khush hua') did nothing to disguise his intention of destroying humanity with cardboard missiles.

Dr Dang of *Karma*, the evil PhD-scientist, who could neither forget the slap on his face by jailor Dilip Kumar nor the fact that he never got tenure.

The bald-headed Shaakaal of *Shaan*, Bond mega-villain Blofeld's wholly owned Indian subsidiary.

The spectacularly named Ajgar Jurrat ('Ajgar' meaning python) of *Vishwatma*, famous more for making 'nanny nanny boo boo' faces at the hero than for causing any permanent damage to humankind.

Acharya-ji of *Ma Kasam*, the undisputed professor of crime as well as music, who never tired of showing how the law dances to his tune by making his pet man in the police wear ghungroos on his feet and walk across the hall swaying his buttocks seductively whenever he came to meet Acharya-ji.

The 'loin' Ajit, the single greatest inspiration for PJs in Indian history.

Where are they today? Have the 'baad maans', the 'Aooooo Lolitaas' and the 'Main Hindustan ko tabah kar doongas' been wiped out in an asteroid strike or have they just stepped out from behind the screen and gone into our public life as politicians, no longer content with the innocent cartoonish buffoonery of yesteryears?

Whatever it be, today's Hindi movies, targeted towards NRIs and A-grade multiplex crowds, have lost all relevance to the common man. Why should the man who toils all day to make a living care for three urban yuppie friends who drive a Mercedes to Goa and then fight among themselves over a trivial issue (*Dil Chahta Hai*) or for two ambiguously gay men trying to get an apartment in Miami (*Dostana*)? Why should the man who wears no underwear care about the peekaboo display of male lingerie of Saif Ali Khan in *Salaam Namaste*? Why indeed?

This disconnect of the common man from the output of the mainstream film industry has led to the rise of alternative entertainment structures in India. Forsaking the claustrophobic world of sepia-toned stylized 'new age' Bollywood, they favour an earthier route to popularity by depicting the ordinary citizen's life, his struggles and his aspirations.

The famous post-colonial theorist, Gayatri Chakravorty Spivak, once asked in an article: 'Can the subaltern speak?' Here the word subaltern was defined as 'a person rendered voiceless by his/her social status.

Well now they can not only speak but speak mellifluously with attendant jhatkas and matkas.

Thanks to the Bhojpuri (a regional language spoken in north-central and eastern India) music industry, the first of our alternative entertainment content producers.

SECTION 1: BHOJPURI BITUWAAS

For those yet to be exposed to the world of Bhojpuri music videos, let me explain what you have missed through a few examples.

Tailors are one of society's most neglected people. Their customers are demanding, impatient and expect premium service, totally oblivious of the tough life these people have.

Bhojpuri artist Lucky Ishtaar (Bhojpuri for 'star') Radheshyam Rasia highlights these challenges in an immensely poetic way through the song 'Rasia Tailor house haw'.

Now Rajkumar Hirani fame may know the travails of engineering students and depict them adequately in 3 *Idiots*, but does he know or even care for the challenges posed by buxom women to a person who stiches blouses for a living?

Radheshyam Rasia does. As the lines go:

Bhari bodon tumhar ba
Maap le le chute paseena
Dahiye chote hamar ba
Pohuche na paaye jo pheeta lagaiyi
Upar se dahiye mutail ba.

In other words, a buxom lady's body is so heavy (especially her upper torso) that the tailor finds it troublesome to measure her with his tape, so much so that he starts sweating profusely.

At another point in the song, Rasiya talks about how some insensitive clients move their bodies uncontrollably while the tailor is taking measurements again oblivious of the poor man's discomfiture.

The tailor's solution to each problem is simple. 'Suth ja suth ja (Lie down lie down),' he exhorts, as he makes his female clients recline on the bench promising them, 'Maap le le hum photaphot. Time laage dus minote.' In other words, a solemn promise is made to measure quickly and do it all (in the style of the average Indian man) within ten minutes. Such is his level of commitment to fast customer satisfaction.

The song (and I so wish I had the technology to embed it in this book) concludes with a message of hope as the beautiful clients dance around with the master tailor while he puts his long tape to good use, wrapping it around the comely lasses while his subordinates move with gay abandon, throwing half-sewn blouses to the wind. The tailor, in the process, becomes one with the dress he has sewn, elevated from being a faceless cog in society's machine to become a vital part of our well-being.

The enduring appeal of Bhojpuri music videos lies not just in it being the voice of the suppressed but also in its finely tuned observations on the minutiae of the social life of the Hindi heartland.

A newly wed wife sings beautifully, 'Duty double sasural mein', talking about her 'double duty' in her father-in-law's house as she services both her husband as well as his brother.

A harried father calls out to his son Anandomohan to take him to the restroom else he will soil himself ('naheen to dhotiyaan mail ho jayeen') but his son is so besotted with his beautiful wife that he ignores his father's biologically motivated calls to satisfy his own biological urges.

An inebriated daily labourer pulls himself up from the gutter and goes to his home hungry, eager for some love, only to be broom-whipped and kicked by his wife even though he romantically keeps singing 'Ramkoli aieee Ramkoli'.

A group of cricket-crazy fans dance hip-hop style to 'Action kar action Dhoni kar jaisan, chowa chakka maare hero jaisan, Dhoni Jharkhand ka hain bara shaan (Do action like Dhoni. Hit fours and sixes like a hero. Dhoni is Jharkhand's star),' laying to rest, once and for all, the canard that cricket is a game for the bourgeois.

The spirit of scientific enquiry is extolled in Guddu Rangeela's famous 'E Buchi bolo seal kaha tooti', where the male singer seeks to find out how the girl Buchi broke her seal (however you may choose to interpret that).

By this time, readers will have understood the very unique ear-to-the-ground perspective to life that Bhojpuri music gives us. Its rhythm beats as one with the heart of the common man, telling his story through its 'random-wa bakchodi' (random conversations) in a way few other embodiments of popular culture, certainly not Bollywood, can hope to do. In that respect, Bhojpuri music videos are historically significant 'living documents' of unparalleled value and historical authenticity.

Consider this: Many centuries later, when scholars try to answer the question as to why India lagged behind other countries in educational indices and they have in their hands two sources – one a government report with statistics and analyses prepared by a bureaucrat, and the other a video of

'Iskool ke tem pe aja gori dem pe (During school time, oh fair girl, come meet me at the dam)' – which one do you think would be considered a more authentic explanation?

The official sanitized version or the subaltern one?

Yep, we know the answer.

The second entertainment structure that has kept alive the spirit of the old Hindi film industry is what is derisively referred to as 'B and C graders' by ignoramuses.

I prefer the less judgemental term 'alternative Bollywood'.

SECTION 2: ALTERNATIVE BOLLYWOOD

In the early '90s, the great Mithun Chakraborty (referred to as Prabhuji by fans like me) left mainstream Bollywood for the Shahrukhs and the Aamirs and migrated to Ooty. Once settled there, an alternative centre for quality Hindi movies organically built itself around him, like a hive around a king bee. Alternative in that it accurately captured the old aesthetic of Bollywood, in sharp contrast to the monster the main branch was slowly metamorphosing into.

Following the philosophy of Henry Ford's assembly line, alternative Bollywood did not so much as make movies but engineer them. A standard revenge plot was used as the underlying framework just like it is done in the product-line engineering paradigm. Minor modifications were added to it to create different products which were then rolled out in minimal time with massive reuse of parts and labour (recycling of scenes, situations, characters and music).

Such was the commitment to speed and to 'Just in Time' delivery of alternative Bollywood that, according to legend, if a fly sat on the camera, it would keep rolling; if the reels of film finished while shooting, then the plot would be so adjusted.

However, there were two things on which no compromises were made.

One was the policy of keeping it 'real' so that the common man could empathize with the plots and the characters.

And the other was to sustain mind-numbing levels of originality such that these movies in no way felt derivative in any shape or form.

How can minor modifications to a basic revenge plot with massive reuse be wildly imaginative and path-breaking?

Read on.

Sher-e-Hindustan

Gulshan Grover plays a villain Choudhury Charannath who, along with his identically dressed sons, rules in the absolutely fascist style of Hitler (incidentally the name of another Prabhuji movie) over a small town. But then one day he is humiliated and jailed by an honest cop played by who else but Prabhuji. In revenge, the evil Charannath vows not to wear clothes. Yes, you read that right. He promises to stay in his underwear for the rest of his life unless his shame is avenged. This of course leads to an immensely dramatic scene when the Gulshan Grover character is walking back from the jail, sans clothes, while his sons run behind him pleading, 'Pitaji aap kapda pahan lijiye (Daddy dearest, please wear clothes).' The scene, in the true tradition of celluloid classics, appeals directly to the audience especially to those of us who have trouble reasoning with obstinate parents.

Retribution, however, is terrible. Just like Draupadi kept true to her oath and washed her hair only after Bheema had brought blood from Dushasana's torn intestines, the unclothed Pitaji ultimately does cover up but not before he strips the entire local police (including Prabhuji) down to their barest of essentials in front of the village. That's not all. After this act of denudation, the evil sons forcibly pierce the noses of the hapless cops and put nose-rings on them. So original was the payback that I am sure Bheema must have said to himself, 'Damn! I wish I had done that to Dushasana before I ate his vitals.'

Diya aur Toofan

One of the persistent complaints that people have about mainstream Bollywood is that there seems to be an almost deliberate rejection of science, as if people who spend their waking hours with lab rats and concentrated nitric acid are not hep and sexy.

Honestly, now tell me, when was the last time that you saw a scientist in a Yash Chopra movie? DJs, call-centre operatives, dancers, musicians, poets, crorepati businessmen, mafia dons and hitmen – we have seen them all.

But a rocket scientist, a brain surgeon, a research assistant? No.

Well, Diya aur Toofan starring Prabhuji and Madhoo, a product of alternative Bollywood, redresses that grievance by putting science back on the centrestage, the place where it belongs. After an honest engineer, Amar (Prabhuji), exposes the criminal activities of the local contractors, he is killed on the night of his marriage.[6]

---

6 In his movies, Prabhuji is typically indestructible. But since in Diya aur Toofan he had taken the avatar of an engineer, a most wimpy incarnation compared to a policeman or a coolie, he had also inherited an engineer's propensity for being handed pink slips by management as well as by God. This explains his death.

In steps science in the form of the great neurosurgeon Dr Vijay (Suresh Oberoi), and his absentminded assistant Gyaneshwar (Kader Khan), who in a salute to Christian Barnard (the guy who did the first heart transplant), extracts Prabhuji's still-alive brain (and what a brain it is), keeps it on a paper plate and puts it into deep-cryogenic-suspended-animation chamber (which looks suspiciously like a toaster-oven but with 'deep freeze' written on its outside) in the hope that one day they will be able to install this brain, like a pen drive, into someone's skull and read the data (the identity of the murderers) stored in it.

They do not have to wait long.

That is because Amar's paramour Asha (Madhoo), when she hears the news of his death, is unable to bear the shock. In crazy transports of passion, she starts slapping/strangling people in her marriage party with such ferocity that her mother dies. Needless to say, unable to bear this additional strain, Asha's brain gets short-circuited and she relapses into infantilism, like the movie's intended audience. Things are brought to a head when, while doing a tandav dance on the steps of a temple, she loses her balance (in more ways than one) and dashes her head on the ground.

Faced with a situation where the heroine is in coma and the hero's brain is in a toaster-oven-cum-deep-freeze machine, Dr Vijay has only one choice. In an operation showed with much scientific precision, Asha's skull, opened up like the hood of a car, is fitted with Amar's brain.

Asha wakes up, not only talking like Prabhuji but also with a haircut just like him. Because Asha is now Amar. This is a fact that Amar understands, with much horror, once (s)he looks down at himself and sees mammaries where once his manly chest was.

At one level, the movie now metamorphoses into a riproaring tale of revenge. Bones crunch, cars fly, screams rend the air and neurons fire. Again and again.

But at another more artistic level, *Diya aur Toofan* becomes something totally different. Capturing the dualism of identity it asks the question that has plagued philosophers from the time of Plato: is it the body that defines the ego or is it the mind? For instance, when Asha seduces one of the villains (played by Mohnish Behl) by rubbing her body against him, is it actually her or is it Amar doing some same-sex male action?

Try finding such depth in *My Name is Khan*.

Exceptional as the movies discussed above are, these are after all still some of the minor achievements of alternative Bollywood. The major ones, that is those that shaped popular consciousness and left an indelible impact on world cinema, are the two movies made in 1997 and 1998 by the Bergman of 'alternative', Mr Kanti Shah.

The first is *Loha*.

And the greatest of them all – *Gunda*.

Let's start of with the one that started it all.

Loha

Quentin Tarantino's *Pulp Fiction* obtained worldwide acclaim for the ingenious way it stitched together multiple story-threads to create a compelling narrative. Kanti Shah goes a step beyond that in *Loha*. He creates two distinct stories – one action-revenge and the other romance-comedy. But then, unlike Tarantino, he does not even try to bring them together.

Instead, he keeps them separate throughout, presenting them as two independent features within the envelope of the same film.

In other words, *Loha* consists of two totally disparate movies, with absolutely nothing in common (no, not even a vague thematic connection), that are interleaved together – thirty-five minutes of action-revenge is followed by fifteen minutes of romance-comedy, which is then followed by another thirty minutes of action-revenge and so on.

Experts have debated the motivations behind this almost unheard-of narrative structure. While no definite answer has ever been agreed upon, the consensus is that this is a device, derived from the best traditions of postmodern art, used by the director to stimulate conversation, discussion and reflection among the audience.

Like the greatest works of beauty, *Loha* is far greater than the sum of its parts, its scope and imagination far exceeding the senseless scenes of cruelty and violence that are the staple of its genre.

Make no mistake. *Loha* does not cheat its audience. It totally gives it what it wants. *Loha* has enough acts of wanton violence and over-the-top action to keep the most hardened front-staller happy. Hands are cut off with a sword, human bombs explode, people get impaled on glass, knives enter stomachs as if they were slabs of butter, necks are twisted, hefty women walk about in two-piece bikinis, the hero (Dharamendra) drags a flying helicopter by a rope tied to it and then tops it off by catching a bullet with his bare hands in the style of Punjab da puttar Shaolin master.

But if *Loha* had stopped here, it would have been a significant achievement on a par with *Sher-e-Hindustan* or *Ma Kasam*. Not more.

However, it is the director's supreme vision and capacity to indulge in allegory that leapfrogs *Loha* to stratospheric levels.

That is because, in the garb of a revenge drama, *Loha* is really an intensely humanist document about relationships.

No, not that between a husband and wife, or between a parent and a child.

Those have been done to death.

Instead, *Loha* is about the interpersonal dynamic between the PhD advisor and his graduate student, the sensei and the kohai.

The movie opens with the akkha Mumbai ka don, harami kasai (bastard butcher) Lukka-bhai, being challenged in his lair by a man who calls himself Tandiya-bhai. It is quickly revealed that Tandiya-bhai was once the mentor and Lukka-bhai was his apprentice. However, subsequently a reversal of fortunes had taken place and now it is the master, fallen on hard times, who is challenging the student for the control of 'Gol Basti'.

Tandiya-bhai starts off the challenge by speaking in impenetrable prose, a standard technique used by PhD advisors to intimidate their students.

'Kauwe ne cheel ka chumma liya aur cheel ne chuhe ka bachcha paida kiya! (The crow kissed the raven and the raven gave birth to a mouse!)'

The student (Lukka-bhai) doesn't get it. He asks his advisor that question which all of us would like to ask our advisors from time to time, but cannot out of fear:

'Khiske re liye kya? (Have you lost it?)'

Seeing the lack of respect from his ex-apprentice, Tandiya-bhai starts driving the sentimental road, pushing for a rapprochement. This he tries to do by reminding Lukka how he had helped the young man in those days when he did not have financial assistance and was exploited by all.

'Yaad hai woh din jab tu din mein boot polish aur raat mein tel maalish kiya karta tha? Mawaali log tujhe chikna chikna bol ke tere peechwade pe haath pherte the. Iske pahele uske haath galat jagah pohuche maine tera haath thaam liya.'

(Remember those days when you used to shine shoes during the day and massaged oil at night? The perverts would call you 'girlie girlie' and rub their hands on your buttocks. Before their hands roamed to the really bad places, I held your hand.)

Lukka-bhai, touched to the quick by this bit of emotional blackmail, takes the opportunity to remind his ex-mentor that his apprentice life was not an easy one. While his advisor was drunk and eating nuts in disreputable places, Lukka was facing the bullets of the police and rival gangs. Transplanting it to an advisor-student context, while the professor, secure with his tenure, was resting on his laurels and had withdrawn into a life of comfort, the student was developing his own research areas and facing hostile reviewers without his advisor's help. And now that the student had created his own domain and community on the docks of Mumbai, he was not going to let his advisor in on programme committees and journal editorial boards.

With his efforts derailed, the master and apprentice then degenerate into poetic abuses and threats, reminiscent of email exchanges between advisor and Phd candidate.

Sample:

'Main dhobi ghaat ke tuteli khaat pe leta leta kar maaroonga, aisi ulti palti karke marega ki tu khoon ki ulti karke marega.'

(Rough translation: The place where clothes are washed, there on a broken bed, I will turn you inside and out so much that you will vomit blood and die.)[7]

---

7 I apologize for losing the beauty of the word-play in the translation.

After this hostile verbal duel, PhD advisor Tandiya makes a vain attempt to usurp his old lieutenant as he launches an assault on his lair. But Lukka is now supreme with all his nuts and bolts in place. As he tells his once master,' Abbe dhille naare, dekha mera nara kitna tight hai. (Your belt is loose. See how tight mine is.)'

Unable to keep his trousers up, Tandiya, the advisor, accepts defeat.

Lukka is heartless. He rubs it into his old boss.

'Abbe o kadwe karele, teri behen marne ke baad teri haalat us AIDS lagi randi ki tarah ho gayi hai, jiske paas kabhi koi giraik nahi jaata... (Oh bitter gourd, after your sister's death your state is like an AIDs-riddled sex-worker who is forsaken by all her customers...)'

Totally broken down, Tandiya offers to relinquish all power and become an apprentice himself, volunteering to do all the demeaning things that graduate research assistants have to do.

'Tu mujhe naukar bana le. Main tera rumaal dhoyega. Chaddi dhoyega. Tera kutta tera ghora banke rahoonga. (Make me your servant. I will wash your hankie. I will wash your underwear. I will be your horse and dog.)'

Reminded thus of his own humiliating status as a graduate student long ago, Lukka-bhai is in no mood to forgive.

Finally, Tandiya-bhai gives up all hope. In one of the most gut-wrenching sequences ever captured on celluloid, he says: 'Ab maar daal mujhe. Main bin petrol ki gaadi aur bin nashe ki taadi hoon. Main woh fateli saadi hoon, jise koi hijdaa bhi nahi pehenta. (Now kill me. I am like a car without gas. I am like whisky without alcohol. I am like a torn sari which even an eunuch will not wear.)'

Rarely has the anguish of seeing one's contribution to one's research domain being relegated to insignificance been so poetically expressed.

Tandiya dies. Shot in the head.

But it is not always the student who emerges as the victor. As part of the perpetuation of the cycle of exploitation, Lukka now becomes the new Tandiya, the professor of sin. This time it is he who takes under his wings a certain promising student, Babu Batla, who has a propensity for wriggling his pectoral muscles when he is excited.

Presently, in a fit of ingratitude, Babu Batla too plots against his advisor, threatening to turn state-witness. But his powers have not been so developed yet as to rise successfully against the master. His rebellion fails totally and he is outwitted by his master, Lukka-bhai.

In another scene of great tragedy, Lukka-bhai, after learning of his student's betrayal, reminisces sadly of how he had developed Batla from an ill-equipped nothing to something.

'Tu kaise bhool gaya jab tu chota sa tha teri itni si thi [showing with his finger a small amount]. Sala mera dudh pee peeke body builder ban gaya aur mujhe dikha raha hain tu? (How can you forget that when you were small, yours was this small. I fed you my milk and made you a bodybuilder. Now you turn against me?)'

Babu Batla is then summarily dispatched to meet the great advisor above. Or in other words, his assistantship is withdrawn. This time it is the advisor whose victory is total.

In conclusion, it is this nuanced portrayal of both sides of a very difficult and little explored relationship inside the larger cocoon of an action movie that makes *Loha* so unique. Of course, there is much much more to this classic, many layers of significance that are only revealed with successive viewings. For instance, there is astute commentary on social distinctions in the evaluation of sexiness (an evil character ogles the daughter of his chauffeur with the line, 'Driver ki beti itni sexy'), reflections on fruits in orifices as in 'Jahaan nimboo naheen ghusta wahaan nariyel ghused dete hain (Where the lemon doth not enter, I can fit in a coconut)', and catty metaphors pregnant with meaning of the sort: 'Tumhari chehra kisi garbhabati billi ki latakti hui pet ki tarah kyon latak raha hai? (Why is your face hanging like the stomach of a pregnant cat?)', a line I always like to use to initiate a conversation with my wife after we have had a fight.

However, despite its obvious greatness history will possibly remember *Loha* more for the fact that it paved the way for *Gunda* than for anything else.

Gunda

The colossus, the baap of all baap movies.

Like *Loha*, *Gunda* is also an action-revenge potboiler. Many of the actors are the same as those in *Loha*. The director and scriptwriter are also the same. The sets appear almost identical in multiple places (for example, an airport tarmac and loading docks form the backdrops for scenes in both movies). There is the recycling of character names. For instance, the corrupt cop is named Inspector Kale in both *Loha* as well as *Gunda*, and the hero in both the movies is called Shankar. Dialogues in *Loha* are referred to in *Gunda*, in the manner that software programmes call external library routines. For example, one of the characters in *Gunda* (Lamboo Atta) reuses a dialogue used by Inspector Kale of *Loha* (both incidentally played by the same actor), in the process welding the two story arcs together in an unprecedented clever way: 'Arre tunhe Kanti Shah ka picture *Loha* naheen dekhi? Usme ek dialogue hain – Chatri hoti hain kholne ke liye, chadar hoti hain odne ke liye aur chokri hoti hain chedne ke liye. (Have you not seen Kanti Shah's *Loha?* That has a dialogue: An umbrella is meant to open, a blanket is meant to cover and a girl is meant to be teased'.)

In this way, *Gunda* represents the high water mark for the production line concept of reuse and optimization, which as we said before was the principle on which alternative Bollywood was founded. Many people have since tried to emulate this manufacturing process but no one has succeeded as spectacularly.

The reason why the success of *Gunda* has never been replicated is because it is no ordinary movie. Just as *Mona Lisa* is no ordinary painting. Sure *Gunda* does have mountains of misogyny, a done-to-death plot, gratuitous violence especially towards women, shocking language and over-the-top acting. Many critics, suffering from an attack of literalism, take everything that *Gunda* has to offer and accept it at face-value without understanding the underlying subtext. It is tragic that while these same critics have no problems in raving about the surreal appeal of Fellini's *La Strada*, they are unwilling to put away their realist sensibilities while evaluating *Gunda*.

If they could they would realize that *Gunda*, intentionally confined by the grammar of popular cinema so as to make the message accessible to the hoi polloi, is actually an allegory where each character represents something larger than just himself.

The mid-'90s were marked by great intellectual ferment and socio-political change in India. With unbridled economic liberalization strengthening the unholy cabal of politicians and moneyed ruffians – this is referred to in *Gunda* as 'aaj gundagiri aur netagiri dono ek hi baap ke do harami aulaad hain (nowadays hooliganism and politics are the bastard sons of the same father)' – the nation witnessed fundamental transformations. This fact was being systematically overlooked by popular escapist entertainment which minted money through vacuous NRI romances, forgetting its solemn duty to be the mirror of its times.

In this context, each protagonist in *Gunda* is presented as a metaphor for the challenges facing India in the 1990s as it captures the essence of an era in the same way that D.W. Griffith's *Birth of a Nation* or Elia Kazan's *On the Waterfront* does.

First there is Bulla, the main evil man. His motto – that has since become a clarion call for youth across the nation – is, 'Mera naam hai Bulla, rakhta hoon main khullaaaaaa (My name is Bulla and I keep it open).' While the literalists interpret this as a vulgar declaration of this man's pride in not wearing underwear, most right-thinking viewers will immediately realize that Bulla represents the 'open' economy – that instrument of the capitalist West – to suck out the lifeblood from the unwashed masses. Yes, Bulla's malignancy represents the depredations wrought by the 'khullam-khulla capitalist system' with its removal of protection for farmers and small industries: in short, the principal villain of the '90s.

Next there is Chutiya, Bulla's hermaphrodite brother who is kept alive through a steady supply of 'London se sex ki goliyan' in the hope that he becomes a 'mard' or man. Chutiya represents the confused generation of the '90s, neutered morally at birth and slowly converted into perverted abomination by the erotic media images on MTV and Channel V (the sex ki goliyan). And the recurrent theme of sex-pills and 'Vitamin sex' is nothing but a thinly veiled reference to the greedy pharmaceutical industries of the West dumping their substandard stock on Third World countries.

Then there is the evil Pote – jo apne baap ke bhi naheen hote (i.e. who is not even of his father). He is an icon for those who revel in wanton violence, whose raison d'etre for living is inflicting pain and suffering – kind of like those who take the lead in acts of terrorism and communal rioting. Their life philosophy is articulated by Pote when he declares with barely controlled glee that 'Hum aise laashein bichha denge jaise kisi nanhen munne bacche ke nanhi si pesaab tapakta hai… tap tap.' When the sound of dead bodies falling on the ground resonates like the pitter-patter of an innocent baby's urine striking the cobble stones – you know that the country is in trouble.

The '90s were marked by a number of ghotalas (financial scandals) initiated by stockbrokers and greedy industrialists, servants of pure avarice, who made common men kneel down and suck their bananas while they aggrandized themselves. This class is crystallized in the character of Ibu Hatela whose patented introduction is: 'Mera naam Ibu Hatela, ma meri chudail ki beti, baap mera shaitan ka chela, khayega kela? (My name is Ibu Hatela, my mother is the daughter of a witch and my dad a disciple of the devil. Wanna have a banana?)' Their natural proclivity to go through the backdoor of the economic system is expressed through Ibu Hatela's repeated use of lines like 'Hum uske pantloon pharenge. Woh bhi peeche se. Angootha lagake. (We will rip his trousers. From behind. And put our fingerprint on it.)'

And of course, the police, which by the '90s had become an extension of the criminal system, does not escape *Gunda*'s angry attention, with Inspector Kale becoming the embodiment of corrupt justice. A picture of total decrepitude is painted in the scene where an honest policeman (the hero's father) accuses Kale of being hand-in-glove with the criminals through the poetic denouncement: 'Lagta hai Bulla ka thook chata hai tu ne, peshaab piya hain uska.' Licking spit and drinking urine. Verily that was the law then.

Finally, the Delhi politician – 'kafan chor neta' – jo Dilli se billi ka dudh peeke aaya hai (he who has come from Delhi after lapping the cat's milk) and Bachchu Bagona represent the cancerous Indian political leadership where friendships are based on mutual benefit (teri biwi uske paas aur uski biwi tere paas soti thi – your wife with him and his wife sleeping with you) and not ideology. These friendships are not permanent, of course, and are quickly transformed into enmity based on the shifting alliances of the criminals that control the politicians. The relationship is symbiotic: while the criminals pay the politicians, the lumpen administrative elements reciprocate by providing them protection. This mutual give-and-take is illustrated in the following line of Chutiya's: 'Yeh jo kaala genda hai na, iske saath jhagra mat kijiye. Kyon ke kanoon aur humare beech yeh ek safed chadar hai. Iske saath jhagra karenge na to kapde dhulenge bharatiya addon pe. (Do not fight with this black rhino-politician. It is he who stands between us and the law like a white sheet. If we quarrel with him, we might be washing clothes inside a government facility.)'

Having created these personifications of India's problems, their dramatic adversary is also presented as a man who hates injustice and is a shining torch for good men and a thorn in the side of the devils: 'Main hoon jurm se nafrat karne waala, shareefon ke liye jyoti, goondon ke liye jwaala. (I hate crime, for the good I am the light and for ruffians I am the pain.')

That man is Shankar (played by Prabhuji Mithun Chakraborty), a coolie at an airport.

He represents the typical hardworking Indian man forced to balance time between an overweight girlfriend, an even fatter sister, an overacting father, alcoholic friends and a pet monkey who can drive a car. It is Shankar and his family who are crushed underneath the 'system' of the '90s – a system that Shankar rises against through the inspirational 'Do chaar chhe aat dus. Bus. (Two, four, six, eight, ten. Enough.)' – reciting of even numbers and concomitant retributory cleansing violence.

This depiction of the eternal conflict between good and evil where each character is an anthropomorphization of historical forces, makes *Gunda* transcend all cinematic formulae, kind of like a Mahabharata of the times.

Just like Mahabharata, *Gunda* is not just about conflict. One will go so far as to say that the conflict is secondary to the human drama. In the best traditions of a Greek tragedy, no one comes unscathed from the *Gunda* experience. While ostensibly the story of a man (Shankar) who loses his father, sister and wife to the evils of society, it is also the cautionary tale of an evil man (Bulla) who, swept away in a maelstorm of revenge and violence, is consumed by the flames of his own rage.

As he once tells Shankar: 'Tujhe jalta bhunta dekhkar hum is tarah khush hote hain jis tarah koi shaitani-type ke bacchen aapne guriya ke haath payer todkar talee marte hainnnnnnn. (Seeing you consumed by the flames of misery I am as happy as those evil-types of babies who clap their hands after breaking their dolls.)'

He first sees his darling sister made lamba (elongated) by arch-rival Lambu Atta. Unable to bear the same pain that he inflicts on others, Bulla laments in an epic scene that would have made the father of Greek tragedy, Euripides, proud: 'Munni meri behen Munni, Munni meri behen Munni, to tu mar gayee? Lambu Atta ne tujhe lamba kar diya? Maachis ki tili ko khamba kar diya? (Munni, my sister Munni. So you are dead? Lambu Atta has elongated you? The match stick has been made into a pillar?)'

If that pain is not enough, he is eaten away every day, piece by piece, by the gut-wrenching sight of his mentally challenged, sexually confused younger brother trying to become a mard (man). Like a helpless elder brother unable to cope with an eternally suffering younger one, Bulla feeds Chutiya sex-pills imported from London. Till one day Chutiya emerges a man – an occasion Bulla celebrates by disco-dancing with eunuchs to the tune of, 'Haye haye mere bhai jawaan ho gya, toota hua teer kaman ho gya. (My brother has become a man, the broken arrow is now a cannon.)' And yet, just when 'tere tube main light aaya tha (the tube light had flickered on)', i.e. he had achieved some level of heterosexual enlightenment, Shankar despatches Chutiya to his maker – as Bulla says, 'Tera fuse uda diya (blew his fuse off),' – by cutting off his organ in a brutal castration scene that even Lorena Bobbit would not have been able to sit through.

Is *Gunda*'s scope just restricted to the cycle of pain and violence? No sir. The canvas is even larger. Sin, redemption and forgiveness. Through acts of bloody retribution, Bulla takes away everything that heroic Shankar holds dear, everything except of course his pet monkey. Shankar's father is hanged from a tree, his sister is brutalized and his girlfriend is skewered with swords. Yet, despite all these blows, Shankar is able to rise above his own desire for revenge to heroically risk his life for sworn enemy Bulla's illegitimate daughter, the one Bulla referred to lovingly as 'haseena ka paseena (my darling's sweat)'.

But Bulla's concept of mercy is very different. He lets God have mercy on his enemies because he himself could not be bothered.

Arch-criminal Lambu Atta, Bulla's sworn enemy, finds himself surrounded by Bulla's henchmen, including the fearful assassin, Kala Shetty. Lambu Atta then asks in vain for mercy:

'Bulla, mere ko mat maar. Mere ko aapna bhadwa bana de. Main ladkiyan supply karta rahoonga aur tu maze lete rahena. Tere ko AIDS se bachane ke liye nirodh ban jayoonga. Towel banke tere kamar se latak jayoonga. Mere ko mat maar. Aur agar maarna hi hai to mujhe chheel-chhaal ke chhakka bana de. Main sari lapet kar tere liye dance karoonga… Gore gore gaal gaal gore gore… (Bulla don't kill me please. Make me your pimp. I will keep supplying you with girls and you keep enjoying. In order to save you from AIDS I shall become a condom. I shall become a towel and hang from your waist. Do not kill me. And if you do want to finish me off, just castrate me and I will become your loyal eunuch. I will wear a sari and dance for you…)'

But mercy does not rain like gentle dewdrops in this case. So vengeful is Bulla that even this heart-rending offer of slavery (which keen readers will note has a marked similarity to a similar sequence between Tandiya and Lukka in *Loha*) cannot save Lambu Atta who gets his maut ka chaanta (death slap) with a swift blow from a knife.

Gunda has left a lasting impression on Indian corporate and pop culture. The Indian outsourcing and client-support industry has consistently found its inspiration from the ultimate 'customer is king' mantra articulated by mega-pimp Lucky Chikna. In an immortal sequence, after catching one of his subordinate sex-workers engaging in lipkam chipki (slang for flirting) with an arbitrary youth instead of servicing a client, Lucky Chikna asks the lady the reason for her slacking off. She says she does not care much for the client who does nothing but tell her to suck his finger (woh buddha kuch karta naheen hai, sirf bolta hain choos choos meri ungli choos). Enraged at this poor attitude to customer service, Lucky Chikna thunders: 'Dhande pe baithi hai to buddha kya, jawan kya, kya chhota kya bara, kya baitha kya khara. (Once you are in business, what do you care if it is young or old, big or small, standing up or sitting down.)'

The impact of *Gunda* on popular culture has primarily been reflected in the number of proverbs and metaphors that it has contributed to everyday language. Be it homilies like 'Roti hoti hain khaane ke liye aur boti hoti hain chabane ke liye, badhsha ki behen ho, ya fakeer ki beti, ek din aati hai marad ke niche bajane ke liye citi' (not translated to avoid the ire of feminists), or slang used in college campuses – 'Tere behen ko kar doonga khullam khullah' (again translation not attempted), or sobriquets like Nirodh Kumar (a character in the movie) that are used to describe children born due to faulty condoms, *Gunda* is part of our lives like no other.

And like all great works of art from Nabokov's *Lolita* to D. H. Lawrence's *Lady Chatterley's Lover*, *Gunda* has been the subject of ceaseless debate and discussions, be it in men's hostel rooms or on Internet message boards. Why does Shankar, a coolie, have a cellphone in the mid '90s? And also a rocket-launcher? Is the relationship between Bulla and Lambu Atta homoerotic? As

Lambu says: 'Bulla ka naam leke tune khada kar diya hai mera. (The sound of Bulla's name has made my "stand up".)' Why did Chutiya, trying to escape from certain death, think that the bathroom was the only place noble Shankar would not look for him? Since the Ambassadors in the movie move about without a driver in sight, are they actually remote-controlled? Why is the Vidhan Sabha and the High Court the same building?

Trying to find the answers to these questions is as futile as trying to reason about the nature of our existence and the ultimate fate of the universe. That is because *Gunda* has been greatly influenced by Dada-ism, a movement of the early 1900s whose principle was the conscious rejection of logic, rationality and conventional aesthetics. Actually the name Bulla is, according to some, a tribute to Bulldada, which means something that is 'brilliant specially because it does not know its own stupidity', with Bulldada itself a term born out of the Dada-ist philosophy.

In conclusion, one can say that there are only two kinds of people in the world. Those who have seen *Gunda*. And those who shall see it.

CHAPTER 12

Five Things That Piss Me Off

HUMAN RESOURCE PERSONNEL

HR: So your salary is fixed at 8.5 lakh per annum.

You: Err... Well... I would like to negotiate.

HR (pretending he has never ever heard the word 'negotiate'): What ate? You ate? That is good.

You: (shifting uncomfortably): I said I want to negotiate.

HR: Ooh negotiate. I am sorry we do not negotiate with terrorists. Haha (evil laugh). No I was just kidding. Joke joke.

You: (shy grin, trying to smile at his lame attempt at comedy)...A lakh would be... emm...

HR: Okay. Let us fix it at 7.5 lakh per annum then. You happy you negotiated. We happy too.

I have come to the following conclusion after much deliberation. Human Resources may be a resource but they are almost never human. Servants of the Dark Lord Sauron with absolute loyalty to the management, these incarnations of evil are forever cutting your privileges (streamlining benefits as they say), losing your paperwork (reducing clutter) and handing out pink slips (strategic resizing).

Okay, these I understand. It is their job to bring death, devastation and lay-offs. Like that of the Grim Reaper.

But can you please tell me why during job interviews they keep on asking the most moronic of questions, to which the only possible answers are dishonest ones.

Take for example, that chestnut which is as old as Middle Earth: 'What according to you are your biggest weaknesses?'

Now you have candidate A who says, 'My weakest point is that I sleep on the job, surf porn when no one is looking and I start looking for the next job within a year of joining.'

That is what I would call an honest answer.

But then you have candidate B who says, 'My weakest point is that I am very detail-oriented and overwork myself till I get it absolutely right.' He knows the trick to answering this hoary question – spin the answer so that it appears as a positive. Well, so does the HR guy taking the interview. If he has any intelligence – and trust me, he is devious – he knows that the answer is prepared and totally bullshit.

Yet you can bet B is the one who gets the job and not the honest man A.

This is precisely why HR people piss me off. They promote disingenuity and hypocrisy, thus furthering the agenda of the devil, in the process essentially turning your interview into a beauty contest.

That's right. Beauty contest. That fine competition where pretty women with white teeth and vacuum compressed brains are compelled to say, 'I will work for world peace,' whereas everyone knows the reason they are there is to land a make-up endorsement contract and a starring role with Emran Hashmi in the next Bhatt flick.

FIRST CLASS IN FLIGHTS

In the 1950s a lady named Rosa Parks refused to vacate her seat for a 'white man' in racially segregated Alabama and set off the Civil Rights movement in the US.

Circa 2003, I was urgently in need of the restroom on a flight on a US carrier. Seeing the Economy Class restroom occupied, and a line in front of the door that looked like the one outside the local ration shop in Kolkata on Saturdays, I made my way to the empty lavatory of the First Class.

Immediately, an inhospitable attendant (the term air hostess is evidently not politically correct) told me that I, humble Economy Class passenger, was not allowed to use the 'higher-class' restroom even though it was empty. The reason given was security though why my using an unoccupied restroom would be dangerous to the safety of the aircraft I did not comprehend. Needless to say, no movement except that raging in my tortured bowels was launched as a result of this.

The caste system/apartheid is well and alive even today. In airplanes, through the First Class system. I have never understood why I should stand back and let another man board ahead of me, just because he is a Platinum First Class customer. I never understand why he gets to walk on the red carpet, why he can jump queues at will, why the airhostess (there I have used the word, so shoot me) smiles more politely at him than at me, and why the need to maintain the exclusivity of his potty corner overrides the urgent biological impulses of the humble coach classer.

Yes, I know. I paid less for my seat. But why does that make me worth less than the First Class passenger. Why do I have to stop in my steps as a premium passenger saunters in towards the boarding entrance? Racists would argue that the white colour of their skin made them 'Premium Members' in the world because of which they deserve the first right over resources, and those of us with coloured skins should stand back when we see them approaching. Replace 'white colour' with 'paid more' and there you have it – First Class.

I shall of course keep protesting this system till the day I attain such a senior position in a company that I myself get First Class tickets as a perk.

Polite Conversation

There was a time when I was single. Parties were then drunk all-men affairs. There would be gratuitous swearing and no-holds-barred puking. Someone would lock himself in the restroom while another would stand on the verandah railing claiming that he would now demonstrate the secret of flight. The romantic guy would recall the girl who left him and start crying. The insensitive dude would say, 'You should have done her when you had the chance.'

The rest of us would concern ourselves with cerebral topics like who was going out with whom, who lost his virginity to his elder sister's friend and which Bollywood heroine was the most generously endowed upstairs. Someone would presently bring out a guitar and we would join in ribald singing inserting meaningful blanks where we wanted, like 'Hothon se chhoon lo tum, mere _____ ko amar kar do' or 'Haathon mein aa gya jo _____ aap ka.'

Then I got married.

Which means we now socialize with other couples, something that is about as much fun as tying a 200-lb weight to your gonads. You are expected to engage in the most polite of conversations, choosing every word you say very carefully. Anything slightly politically incorrect is met with uncomfortable silence and a subtle accusatory glance as if to say, 'A few more of that and you are not getting invited back.' As a single man, I never cared what people thought of me. As a respected married member of the society, I now realize my reputation is everything. So I admire the hostess's new garden and especially the fresh petunias, appreciate the newly acquired furniture, discuss the advantages of the Atkin's diet over the South Beach diet and ask her for the recipe for this delicious lemon meringue pie.

But sometimes during a lull in the conversation, my eyes look at a spot in the wall and I imagine myself getting up, as I used to in times gone by, and bawdily sing ' Hothon pe bas tera _____ hain, tujhe _____ mera kaam hain...' (gaps inserted to impart a deeper meaning).

Presently I am brought back from my reverie by one of the guests, one half of a couple, politely asking me whether I have ever gone hiking near Mount Hood in Oregon.

I shake my head benignly as I take a sip of oxidizing green tea and marvel about the flavour and aroma.

The Flush

I have developed something which I can only characterize as a pathogenic hatred of commode flushes. As if my social life isn't complicated enough, it invariably happens that when I go to someone's house there is something about the flush that just doesn't seem to work.

A plumber once told me in Kolkata that every flush is like a child. That is, each needs to be treated differently. Some need gentle pats with the hand to make them work while some need a savage box of the ear. Then there are others who need to be coaxed several times patiently before they pass water through the bowl. Now the problem when you go to someone's house is that you do not know which personality type the 'nanha munna' flush in question falls under.

So there you are having done what you went to the bathroom to do. You pull the flush and then nothing happens. Or worse, an apologetic tiny spurt of water tinkles down, like teardrops on the cheeks of time. Needless to say, it does nothing to discharge its primary purpose – to wash down the waste. Panicking, you jam the flush again. And again, nothing. Tinkle tinkle.

Right then there is someone knocking on the door asking, 'Is anyone there?'

And this is not the worst that can happen in someone's toilet.

The worst. What would that be?

Let me tell you. Sometimes, and it does not happen always, but sometimes the devil possesses the bowl or perhaps something gets stuck in the plumbing. It is then that when you flush, rather than the water spiralling down it gurgles up, overflowing the rim. Yes I will spare you the details but you get the 'flow' here, don't you? This is as close to a glimpse of Dante's fifth circle of hell that you will ever get to see while alive.

Then of course there are the airport flushing systems. Indian places are better in that respect. They have a small chirag-e-Aladdin which contains water with a broom right next to it. I like that. It is simple and clear.

The problem is when technology makes its appearance. As it does in many international airports. Rather than having a big prominent 'flush lever', they make things space-age by having a button, one that is often so friggin' miniaturized that I sometimes have difficulty locating it. Some make things even worse by having exclusively motion-activated flushing systems. Maybe it is just me but I find that the sensors often do not seem to work as they are supposed to and I have been in situations standing in a cubicle, with people waiting outside impatiently coughing, shaking my unclothed butt desperately in an obscene attempt to trigger the sensor so that my stuff can go down where it must. But to no avail.

I really hate flushes. Honestly I do.

CALLING CUSTOMER SERVICE

Automated Voice: 'Thank you for calling company XYZ. Please listen carefully as our menu options have recently changed. If you want to sign up as a new customer, press two. If you are an existing customer, press three.'

I press three.

'If you want to upgrade your plan, say 'Upgrade my plan'. If you want to check your latest balance, say 'Check latest balance'. If you want to cancel your plan, then... oh wait... there is static on the line... Dialtone.

Okay, I made the last message up. But there is one thing I have noticed. The automated menu often does not give you any option for talking to a live customer representative. However, that is exactly the reason why I dialled the customer service number in the first place. It's almost as if the company does not want you to find them. I wonder why!

Of course, I know the tricks. The first trick is not to say anything. That is when the artificial intelligence recognizes that you are a stubborn bastard who is giving it the silent treatment, absolutely determined to speak to live support. At this point, it transfers you to a customer service rep.

Some automated systems do not even take that hint. They will repeat, 'I am sorry, but I did not understand your response,' pushing you further on the path of exasperation.

Realizing that the automated voice is not going to give you the option, you play your last card. Dial 0. If there indeed is a live operator, this will usually connect you to one. If nothing happens, then you are out of luck.

I am however lucky this time. I am connected.

But do I hear a sweet friendly voice immediately? No I do not.

Automated voice: In order to serve you better, we would need you to enter certain details of your account.

Serve me better! Hah! Considering that you have done absolutely nothing in terms of providing service so far, that's pretty ironic. But then again paraphrasing Alice from *Alice in Wonderland*, you can always do more than nothing.

Then the automated voice insists on pestering me for every bit of information that it possibly can – my mother's last name, my full name, my full address, my birthdate, when I lost my virginity and with whom. If one didn't know better, one would think that the company was just trying to waste my time and get me to hang up.

After about six to seven minutes of this 'getting to know ya' for the sake of 'better service' the voice says:

'Transferring your call… Your call may be recorded for quality control and training purposes. Your average waiting time is thirteen minutes. Your call is important to us. All our customer service agents are busy with other customers.'

There is a big lie here.

That my call is important to them. Of course it is not. The reason is simple. I am an 'existing customer'. If I had pressed option number 2 (sign up as new customer) I am sure a representative would have immediately been with me. But since I am not a prospective 'bakhra' (goat), my call is about as much important to the company as religious freedom is for the Taliban.

Incidentally, the reason why the customer service agent is busy with other customers is because the company has very few agents and many irate customers. My business important to them, my foot!

After a wait time of about twenty-five minutes, during which I am entertained by uplifting music, punctuated by an automated voice that reminds me how important my call is and how sorry they are for keeping me on hold, a human voice comes on at the other end of the line.

Now what does that voice make me do? It makes me repeat all the information I had already given them.

Serve me better? Double hah.

The fun is just getting started. Customer representative listens to me for three minutes, then decides it is not his division.

He then puts me on hold and Kenny G plays again.

After seven minutes, the call goes to someone else, who, surprise of surprise, asks me for my personal data once more and makes me repeat my complaint.

Then she says, 'Please wait while I pull up your account information. While we wait, have you heard of the special promotion we are running? If you want, we can add these value-based services to your account.'

The height of chutzpah, these people are not above taking advantage of a call to customer service to hawk their products. I swallow my rage as the data is pulled up, coincidentally not before the marketing speech finishes.

Customer rep then profusely apologizes for the inconvenience and then either politely tells me to stuff the complaint up my behind or gives me a docket number and asks me to call back in ten days.

Ten days! And that too call back when all of us know what a pleasant experience that is.

I show my indignation.

The person at the other end of the line is probably smiling soundlessly. I ask to speak to the supervisor.

Big mistake!

Sure sir, he says. And immediately puts me on hold.

Again I have two options.

Option 1 is to hang up and pray to God the problem resolves itself. I would take this option if I was smart. However, I am not. Otherwise why would I have been on the line for forty-five minutes, engaged in what I knew from the minute I called, was an exercise in futility?

So I take Option 2. Keep on waiting. After ten minutes, the supervisor comes on the line. Yep. I do it. Again. Explain the whole problem that is.

He apologizes for the inconvenience, explains this is all part of the process and that the customer is the most important to them.

As I listen to that patently insincere, rehearsed bit of crap, I am reminded of that line from *As Good As It Gets*:

'Where do they teach you to talk like this? In some Panama City "Sailor wanna hump-hump" bar, or is it getaway day and your last shot at his whiskey? Sell crazy someplace else, we're all stocked up here.'

Of course I do not say anything like this since the last thing I want is a 'system error' charging a few thousand bucks for a service I never used. I politely try to reason with the supervisor and realize that I was having better luck convincing the automated voice.

I play tough, subtly threatening to take my business elsewhere. The supervisor tells me, 'Your business is important to us, sir.' This is customer rep speak for 'Do I sound like a give a rat's ass? Our commission is made on acquisition and not on retention.'

I then plead. And finally give in. No, that's not an accurate representation of my surrender. I finally let go like the sphincter of a man hanging from the gallows.

I prepare to put down the receiver.

Not soon enough though. As the phone disconnects, the voice takes a parting shot: 'We enjoyed serving you today, sir. If you would kindly take two minutes of your time to fill out a customer satisfaction survey...'

With the phone firmly on the hook, I bury my face in my hands and bawl like a baby.

CHAPTER 13

How Bollywood Made Me What I Am

I wore the *Maine Pyar Kiya* cap with FRIEND written on it, many years before Ross, Joey and Rachel popularized the word in a totally different context. The Deepak Tijori hand-gesture from *Aashiqui* became a bad habit of mine in high school. The Bachchan shuffle was executed perfectly through repeated practice. So was the Madhuri Dixit Dhak Dhak bust shake from *Beta*.

You read that right. Even the Madhuri bust shake. That is because Hindi movies have influenced me. A lot. Not just in the way I have dressed, talked and shouted 'Oye Oye Oye Ooo Waaa', but in the way that I have behaved, dreamt and fantasized. Had it not been for Bollywood I perhaps would have been a very different person from what I am today.

As I guess would have been so many others.

My masala influences have been many and it would take a lifetime to acknowledge them all.

So let me concentrate on just a few, those very few celluloid classics that have had the most impact on me, shaping, inspiring, guiding and moulding my personality.

No wait. 'Acknowledge' is not the word.

Derama naheen hain is mein.

So let me put it like this.

In this chapter, I virtually touch the feet of the following movies, look towards the camera and bellow with glycerine-induced tears streaming down my cheeks (to the sound of thunder), 'Yeh hai meri shraddhanjali' (This is my tribute).

(Musical flourish.)

Aatish – Feel The Fire (1994)

You live in a men's hostel. After a night out on town, you return to a darkened room and flip the switch on. Then stand back startled as you see your roommate, with a magazine of an unclad woman, lying on your bed. Before your mind can comprehend what is going on, there is a blur of activity, your friend adjusts his clothing and jumps off his place of repose looking sheepish and embarrassed.

There are two options open to you. If you have no sense of hostel life or for the feelings of your roommate, you berate him for doing 'dirty' things on your bed.

If, however, you are a humanist with a deep empathy for all, you channel Baba (Sanjay Dutt)from Aatish repeating what he said to Nawab (Aditya Pancholi) after coming out of jail and discovering his friend, in a pathetic sub-human state, gulping down inedible food all alone in an abandoned garage on a rainy day.

'Akele akele?' (Rough translation: Doing it alone? Or more accurately, in the context of the movie, 'Started off without me?')

Aatish, Sanjay Gupta's maiden directorial venture, is remarkable.

No, not just because it is possibly the only Hindi movie ever made where the hero is taunted by the villains by the singing of 'Baa baa black sheep, have you any wool?' (Thankfully, the hero in question is Sanjubaba and not any of our holistically hirsute hairy-fairy heroes in which case the significance would have been definitely sinister).

No, not just because it was perhaps the first movie I know that had a song the lyrics of which had to be changed because it offended religious 'sentiments' ('Ya Mustafa ya Mustafa' became 'Ya dilruba ya dilruba').

No, not just because IIT professors have used its action sequences as reference to set question papers for mechanics – 'A man whose mass is m runs at x m/sec and jumps of a building of height h_1, spinning at an angular velocity of w while his body makes an angle θ with the vertical. He fires a bullet from his gun at an initial velocity u and with an accleration f. If the accleration due to gravity is represented as g, what will be the velocity of the bullet after t seconds?'

And no, it is not because *Aatish* had chawanni dialogues like 'Chal Nawab, tere payer ke hisaab barabar karne ke liye (Let's go to settle the account on your leg)', when Baba finds out that the villain Kaniyaa had chopped off Nawab's legs as an act of retribution.

Or because it had the anthem of insomniacs with angina: 'Dil dil dil, main saari raat na soya. Main kya karoon?' (Heart heart heart, I have not slept the whole night. What to do?)'

Aatish is remarkable because of its depiction of the purest form of 'feel the fire' love between man and man. Namely that between partners-in-crime Baba and Nawab. With movies like *Brokeback Mountain* subsequently putting a homoerotic subtext on every man–man lovey-dovey relationship, *Aatish* harks back to a purer, more innocent time when a man could, as Nawab does to Baba, sensually massage his biceps and say, 'Kya body hai tera, Baba.' Or where Baba could look deep into the eyes of Nawab and say, 'Tu shola hai aur main aatish,' without people sniggering behind their backs and exchanging knowing glances.

Because that is exactly what we, engineering college boys, used to do. In that we would touch and admire each other's muscles (biceps,triceps and even quadriceps), give friendly hugs, cuddle up, feel each other's fires – stuff that if now revealed would open us to judgements about our sexuality.

And today, older and wiser and respectable family men ourselves, when we watch *Aatish* again we see ourselves reflected in the way we used to be – frustrated, deprived of female company, desperate to no longer do it 'akele akele', on the verge of 'khud khushi'(suicide) from years of 'khud khushi'(auto pleasure). It is then that *Aatish* becomes less a movie and more a personal document, an affirmation of our identities and the purity of our pasts.

For me, however, the most personal *Aatish* story is from 1994, on a day that was perhaps one of the lowest in my life. The Joint Entrance Examination results had come out and my rank was much lower than what I had expected. Barely controlling my tears I sat on the ground when a friend from school, who knew what had happened, came running. 'What the hell happened?'

With my voice choked with emotion, all that I could do was repeat what *Aatish*'s villain, the one-eyed, eternally luckless Kaaniya (Gulshan Grover), used to say while pointing at his forehead, his voice (like mine) soaked with disappointment and anger:

'Kismaat... (Bad luck...)'

Yes. It's very touching. In all sorts of ways.

Mohra (1996)

There is one thing I have always been rather good at. That is dancing dhinchaak disco style. People ask me the secret of my moves, how my legs, butt and back are so marvellously coordinated at all times.

I smile enigmatically.

Of course I am not going to tell them my secret, just like a beauty will never reveal her ghane kaale baalon ki raaz.

Okay, maybe I will. My dancing style has a simple algorithm which was taught to me during my engineering college ragging.

Standing in front of a group of seniors on orientation day, I was asked to dance.

When I said I did not know how to, a senior asked me to imagine there was a virtual pencil stuck up my ass and that I had to write my name with that virtual pencil on a virtual blackboard.

The moment I started following his instructions my buttocks, waist and legs magically collaborated to execute some out-of-the-world steps.

This move, the senior told me, was known as the Akshay Kumar Mohra move and this he knew was how the 'Tu cheez badi hai mast mast' dance could be faithfully replicated.

It has since become the style that I have faithfully copied. But I didn't go to see Mohra for that dance. No. I went in because one day a friend, whom I shall refer to simply as X (in case his wife should read this book), told me:

'Dude. You have got to go and see *Mohra*. They got Raveena wet. I mean totally wet. You cannot miss this.'

Now at that age, I would not go much by Ebert and Roper or the *New York Times* review, nor was I overly worried about plot or character development. If the heroine was shown getting wet, that in itself was worth the price of admission – a total thumbs-up for me.

In the '90s the 'get wet' queens ruled. Wherever they went, it did not just rain. It poured. So much so that I often used to wonder whether their roles were defined in terms of the number of lines of dialogue they would get to speak or in the terms of the litres of water that would be unloaded on them. And Raveena, with her wet-wet number 'Kabhi tu chaliya laagta hai' from *Patthar Ke Phool* had firmly entrenched (or should I say en-drenched) herself in the Wet Wet Hall of Fame.

So, given the ringing endorsement, of my friend there was no way I was not going to see *Mohra*.

Raveena did not disappoint me. No, she did not.

Nothing about *Mohra* disappointed me.

And how could it?

It had Akshay Kumar, Bollywood's Khiladi (unrelated factoid: In the hip-hop way of life, a 'ladies' man' is called a player), who from beginnings as an Indian James Bond in *Mr Bond*, where he had bikini-clad ladies dancing to the song 'Handsome man' while he cavorted in speedos, had emerged as one of the most dependable action stars of the era.

It had Suniel (the artist formerly known as Sunil) Shetty who had become a great favourite of mine since his *Gopi Kishan* days, principally for his 'Hai huku hai huku hai hai' cavortings in a

T-shirt that had SODA written on its front (I have spent many hours ruminating whether it is the acronym for Statement of Demonstrated Ability) and also for dancing to another song whose lyrics went 'Main bhakt hoon Hanuman ka. Ayoonga na tere haath mein (I am a devotee of Hanuman. I will not be ensnared by you).'

It had the redoubtable Paresh Rawal playing Kashinath Sahu, the cowardly cop with a fondness for cross-dressing as Gol Chowki-waali Champa Rani whose 'golai' (roundness) is accentuated by the tennis balls that are stuffed inside his blouse, the ones that had the unfortunate tendency of falling out when he was deep undercover.

It had a surreal climax where the villain, instead of trying to make a getaway, wasted vital time trying to get the hero cop Amar (Akshay Kumar) to take off his trousers, laughing manically and shouting 'Patloon utaro (Take off your pants)' as the audience sat in shocked silence.

But most importantly, it had an amazing twist – something that was so surprising and shocking that it affected me profoundly. Namely, Pankaj Udhas's syrupy voice being used as playback for gruff he-man Suniel Shetty.

I honestly never saw that coming. My faith in humanity was shaken. Forever.

Gupt: The Hidden Truth (1997)

Since the professor who taught us Digital Circuits in consecutive classes did not take attendance, we used that block of free time to slip out of college and catch movies. It was one such afternoon that three of us friends made it to the theatre to watch the just-released Gupt.

We had been warned of a scalper who, if you did not buy tickets from him, would blurt out 'XYZ did it' (*Gupt* is a murder mystery) as a means of extracting revenge for the failed transaction.

Though we managed to safely avoid this villain, our cinema-watching experience was far from perfect. For one, there was a drunk sitting at my friend's side, who was periodically threatening to puke on him (he may also have been a movie critic), in response to which my friend kept pulling at my sleeve, begging me to change places.

Being a good friend, I ignored his entreaties.

Contributing to the lovely atmosphere were a group of two boys and two girls sitting behind us. From their school uniforms, it was obvious they had bunked school.

If that was not distasteful in itself the boys kept passing comments throughout the movie. Like when Sheetal (Monisha) unzipped her jacket seductively before the song 'Bechainia', schoolboy 1 told schoolgirl 1:

'See that. Just see that. One day you too will have a body like her's.'

Or like when Sahil Sinha (Bobby Deol) got into a fight with a scary-looking guy in jail (the prison set-up looked very similar to the Devil's Island of *Papillon*, a fact perhaps acknowledged in a very Quentin Tarantino-style by naming the place in *Gupt*, Shaitaan Kothi), schoolboy 2 told schoolboy 1:

'Hey, that dude is as hairy as your dad.'

I am sure you understand how difficult it was to concentrate on the movie at hand in the midst of all these distractions. This is why when I first watched *Gupt* I was not so impressed. Except of course by Sahil's wardrobe, containing by 'black with red roses' printed jackets (many years later, I saw a similar design in a female lingerie catalogue) and also by a few well-written dialogues which I memorized for use in appropriate situations.

Like, 'Main ek salesman hoon. Ishq aur mohabbat ka salesman. Tum jaisi khoobsoorat ladkiyon ki zaroorat puri karta hoon aur woh bhi muft mein. Mere paas premshastra ka gyan hain. Agar mere honth tumhare honthon se takra gaye to samajh lo tumne prem shastra mein awwal number pa lee ho. Awwal number paana chahogi na?'

(I am a salesman. A salesman of love. I exist to satisfy your needs and that too for free. I am skilled in the art of love. If my lips should make contact with yours, consider you have emerged a topper in the art of love. Do you want to be a topper?)

It was only later, after multiple viewings of this classic, that I came to appreciate its genius. It was then that *Gupt*'s effect on me was fully realized in that the way I looked at mystery-solving totally changed.

Having read Arthur Conan Doyle and Agatha Christie, I had thought of the art of solving mysteries as comprising deduction, induction, use of deep insights into human nature and varied other intellectual gymnastics.

Everything I had believed to be right, I found now, was wrong.

In *Gupt*, Sahil Sinha's stepfather, the governor, is murdered and Sahil is set up for the crime. Escaping from jail, he embarks on a mission of back-to-the-wall detection as he tries to uncover the real killer. In order to do so, he does not sit on a couch and smoke opium in Sherlockian style, nor does he twirl his moustache Poirot-like.

Instead he catches hold of Suspect i, punches him repeatedly till Suspect i says, 'I did not do it. But I know that Suspect (i+1) did it.' At which point of time, Sahil Sinha goes to Suspect $(i+1)$ and the loop is repeated with $(i=i+1)$ till all suspects are exhausted.

So impressed was I by this direct action approach that I have subsequently adopted this as my philosophy of research. While my colleagues favour the use of brain and intellect and theory, I go about my work *Gupt*-style, throwing fists, banging hands into shelves, and putting the issues into boiling water, hoping that the solution lies right in front of me, like it did for Sahil Sinha who found out, after inflicting pain on suspects (and the audience), that the devious murderer had left his/her picture at the scene of the crime.

Unfortunately, I have not been as successful as Sahil Sinha, perhaps because my life's script is not written in Bollywood. But that has not stopped me from blowing up anything and everything in search for a solution.

This is not, however, the only way *Gupt* has remained alive in my life.

For instance, even today, when my wife finds a password-protected folder on my machine under C:\old program files\project5\tmp and asks me what these are, I repeat a line that Dr Gandhi (Kulbhushan Kharbanda) says before he is murdered, a line that also represents the sentiments of many public servants when served with an RTI (right to information) order:

'Kuch baatein (pause) gupt raheni chahiye.'

(Some things are better kept hidden.)

Tahalka (1992)

I have always been a political animal. Whether it be at college eating bread soaked in rasogolla syrup or later in graduate school sipping a latte, I never let an opportunity for political debate go by as I blow much hot air (through my mouth, just for the sake of clarification)and deplete much ozone.

One of the red-button issues that always gets me passionate is the threat posed by a certain nation to our north, one that refuses to recognize our territorial integrity, one that creates bases ('string of pearls') encircling the country, providing financial aid and weapons to our other adversaries, a danger whose full magnitude is rarely recognized.

No points for guessing which country I am talking about.

Dongri-La.

In *Tabalka* Anil Sharma laid bare the sinister designs of this country, 'jinki hawas ki had apne sarhadon se nikal kar Hindustan ke hadon mein ghusne ki koshish main rahee hai (whose lustful designs seek to penetrate Hindustan)', as the voice-over at the start of the movie says.

Dongri-La, I was told, is ruled by a dictator, the sitar-playing 'Shamosha Shashaa'-singing Dong (played by Amrish Puri), whose motto 'Uparwala wrong ho saakta hai par Dong kabhi wrong naheen hota (God may be wrong but never Dong)' encapsulates a political philosophy which considers religion to be the opium of masses and negates the infallibility of God. Anybody who is even a minute late for an appointment or shows any form of dissent by not saying, 'Bukchika Bum Bum Long Live Dong,' or by protesting in a city square is immediately shot. The evil Dong's minions infiltrate India to capture girls from Hindustan out of which the voluptuous ones are kept in his gulag where 'they do anything Dong asks them to' (presumably make lead-filled toys or sell fake drugs among other things) while the other ones he harvests for their kidneys and hearts.

Sick and tired of their nefarious activities, a great patriot, Major Krishna Rao – whose red-hot passion for the nation is manifested through lines like 'Badalne waale hum cheez naheen, arre hum mard hain, koi kameez naheen (I don't change, I am a man, not a shirt)' – decides to assemble a crack team of India's commandos (played by Naseeruddin Shah,Javed Jaffrey, Aditya Pancholi and Ekta). Assisted by disgraced super-soldier Dharam Singh (played by Dharmendra who sings 'Put on the ghungroo on my feet and watch the deraama') and dissidents like King Cow (Prem Chopra), these commandos then travel to Dongri-La to assassinate Dong, a mission that leads to betrayal, songs, urination for the sake of the nation, the blowing up of an entire mountain and the discovery of traitors inside Hindustan who are in the pay of Dongri-La.

In conclusion, if *Tahalka* was just history and the inspiration behind the naming of a certain investigative newspaper, things would actually be fine.

But it is not. Because the malignancy of Dongri-La has remained alive despite the heroism of Major Krishna Rao's team as even today many inglorious acts (like repeatedly trying to re-draw India's borders) are perpetrated by Dong's successors 'Hu'-ever they may be.

This is why *Tahalka* remains relevant for all time, continually shaping the political perspectives of countless Hindustanis like me.

Clerk (1989)

Sometime around when I was fourteen I became somewhat of a rebellious teen, questioning authority and all accepted wisdom. I fell in with the bad boys of school and began wondering why the hell I was slogging away for five more marks in Bengali when I could be doing something much more pleasurable – like watching *Street Hawk* on Sunday mornings or playing cricket till six-thirty in the evenings.

The bouquet of methods the powers-that-be used in order to keep me on the straight and the narrow included threats like the one a teacher in school was fond of repeating:

'Do you know what happens if you do not stay on the top of class? Unemployment that's what! Or perhaps at best a clerk in some office. You need to become a doctor or engineer if you want to survive in today's world.'

'So?' I thought. 'Being a clerk does not sound bad. Go to work. Sit at a desk. Copy stuff around. Come back. Watch *Street Hawk* on Sundays.'

And so I continued on my merry ways, keeping my book open but looking out through the window at the neighbour's kid flying a kite on the roof, oblivious of the fate that may befall me for not memorizing the annual bajra yield of Uttar Pradesh in the year 1987.

Then I saw *Clerk*.

It was more than an intervention. It was like God speaking to me from behind a burning bush.

In the movie *Clerk*, a dangerously close-to-reality story of corruption in defence contracts, Bharat (played by Manoj Kumar) is a clerk in the said ministry, of course not for lack of academic skills (he is the college topper) but due to the debilitating poverty of his father, Satyapati (played by Ashok Kumar).

And what a hellish life he has, a condition of subhuman existence captured by the song he sings 'Aansoo peeyun kyon ki main ek kelerk hoon... (I drink my tears 'cause I am a clerk...)'

For good reason too! At work, his boss taunts him by whispering viciously, for no good reason other than to humiliate him, 'Tum ek mamooli clerk ho' (You are an ordinary clerk). At home, he has no money to treat his father or pay for his younger brother's education, or for his elder brother's prosthetic foot (he is an injured fighter pilot who hobbles on one leg). His elder brother's wife has to sell her blood every month so that the clerk can go to bed on a full stomach, even though her husband suspects her of spousal malfeasance mainly because she goes to the blood bank dressed, for some reason, in her 'suhaag raat waali sari'. If that is not bad enough, the clerk Bharat's slippers are always torn as he labours through life of a state of permanent depression ('phati hui chappal, bujhi bujhi surat').

Seeing the state of the poor Bharat, I was really scared. No way could I allow myself to become like that. Since I was an only child I wouldn't even have a bhabhi who could be counted upon to sell her blood for my supper. So I would be even worse off than Bharat if I became a 'kelerk'.

I had to study. No two ways about it.

Also, I could not let myself become a doctor, since they are, as shown in *Clerk*, merciless worshippers of Mammon, who (horror of horrors) demand fees for their services.

Exhibit 1, your honour.

Bharat's father Satyapati is having angina pains. Younger brother returns but without a doctor. Why? Because the doctor has told him, 'Main doctor hoon, mujhe fees chahiye.'

Well, screw the doctor anyway. Who needs medical science when you love your country? Seeing his father clutching his heart in pain, Bharat realizes that he has his dad's medication in his hand.

Batteries.

For his pacemaker perhaps?

No way. Patriots don't need pacemakers.

So then why the dry cell?

Hah. You never saw this coming. Bharat pops them into the record player. It starts playing the old Azaad Hind Fauj anthem, 'Kadam kadam badaye ja'. Before you can say 'Cholesterol', Satyapati is on his feet with the surge of patriotic electricity unleashed by the song jump-starting his faltering heart in a way no defibrillator can. Not only is he fit as a fiddle but soon he is singing and marching again with the whole family joining him.

Which just goes to show what my uncle used to say. That the pharmaceutical lobby in collusion with medical providers is making us buy pills we don't need and then charging us 'fees' for these services, when all that is needed is some strong will to cure all diseases.

My career choices reduced by this indictment of the medical profession, I had no option but to become an engineer.

At least, if nothing else, I would be able to fix the record player.

CHAPTER 14

1-900 Hotties

When Rahul came to the US to do his Master's in Computer Science (what else could he do, being a desi he had been programmed at birth to do one) he had the standard immigrant dream – dollars, a house, two cars and two kids.

Well, not quite.

Sure, he wanted all these things but what he wanted most of all was to live out his fantasy. In his dreams, life in the US was 'as seen on MTV' – a never-ending hedonistic pleasure-trip of bikini-clad girls dancing on the beach and partying the night away in a psychedelically lit disco.

And so the day he got admission into graduate school in the US he thought that the gateway to heaven had finally opened.

However, the educational system brought him back to reality with harsh lashings of its whip. He found out soon enough that the only thing he could play around with was the Linux kernel, the only promiscuous mode he would ever see would be in computer networks. It was not that he did not try — he and a couple of his friends took the campus bus and went to a bar to 'pick up blondes'. All that happened was that they sat there, ordered the cheapest beer they could (they had wisely come during 'happy hour'), drank alone, stared at each other, ogled the ladies who did not seem to even look at them through their cascading locks of gold, and came back even more frustrated than before

His friends still went to bars regularly; one of them even took the phone number of a girl he danced with on New Year's but, well, that was all he could do. Rahul, not being as hopeful as his mates, had stopped frequenting bars and pubs. There was no way he could ever get noticed. It did not matter if you were black or white, sang Michael Jackson, but according to Rahul when it came to hitting on chicks in bars, it did matter if you were brown.

His friends disagreed, of course, and they went toiling in their endeavour, working out heavy at gyms, drinking protein shakes and ordering $2.99 e-books titled *How to bed any woman*. *Yes any woman*, which they used with as much religious diligence as Straustroup's C++ reference and the Java documentation – however, with much lesser success.

As Chokalingam (who thought that the line 'I am Chuck and I like f**ck' made him irresistible to women) was fond of saying about his misadventures: 'The requirements were well-defined. The design was right. My implementation however was buggy. Total project failure da. Total failure.'

And so life went on.

Rahul stayed in a loft with two other desis. While the American students downstairs would start partying from Thursday night he had to be content with peering down at the girls making out with the guys on the porch and listening to the cries of passion emanating through the thin wooden walls while he gulped down cold vegetable noodles from his small white bowl.

He had tried chatting with girls on the Net but he could not trust anything on chat – it was obvious that the girls who wanted to talk 'hot' were not really girls at all but similarly frustrated desi men. And the girls, the very few that there were, would be immensely boring and trying to make 'friendship' of the long-term variety – something that Rahul did not have the time for. I mean, after nights of endless coding he reasoned that talking about his family, his hobbies and his zodiac sign was a waste of effort when all he wanted was to get down to business with an opening line like 'So what are you wearing?'.

Our story is about one fine night. A Saturday night, in fact.

At 2:30 Rahul had returned from school. The code had core-dumped without any explanation, his advisor was breathing down his neck, the Chinese teaching assistant had put a B on an assignment unfairly. A night like any other night, Rahul thought, as he threw his head back on the torn couch(brought two months ago from the sidewalk where it had been abandoned by its owners, for good reason), and tried to collect his thoughts. His apartment mates Rohan and Vikas had gone shopping in the evening and God knows where they were so late – maybe sleeping.

In a reflex action he started surfing the channels on his TV – was there anything good on? 'Real Sex' on HBO perhaps? *Bedroom Eyes* if he was lucky?

Nope.

HBO had some old Tom Hanks movie playing and

everywhere else there was nothing but infomercials – the fat burning grill, the get-rich-by-selling-real-estate, the Christ-is-waiting-to-rescue-your-soul, the amazingly loaded laptop that would be sold out in ten minutes.

As Rahul kept flipping channels mindlessly, suddenly his reverie was disturbed by a sharp female voice.

He looked up.

'Are you tired?' asked a heart-wrenchingly beautiful blonde.

Yes he was, Rahul thought. Most definitely.

She was then joined by another bountiful babe who pouted: 'Are you lonely?'

Yes he was – yes, he most certainly was.

A brunette with a generous visual display unit piped in: 'We are waiting for your call, big boy.'

Then a voice-over said encouragingly: 'We have real girls in your area who want to meet you and have a good time. Call 1-900-HOTTIES to blow your mind.'

Cut to the three girls now slithering among themselves: 'What are you waiting for? The night is still young. 1-900-HOTTIES...'

The phone lay on the adjoining couch. Rahul looked at it longingly. Was this the real way to meet local girls? Of course not, this is a phone sex line; he knew all about them.

He flipped the channel again – a Discovery channel special on the mating habits of the Siberian bear.

He looked at the phone again.

Why not try it?

What if the girls from his university were doing it for money?

What if he got lucky?

And at worst, there would be a real girl talking dirty on the other side – just the perfect arrangement. No aggravation of conversation, just jump to the good parts, no threat of rejection, total confidentiality – and he had caught the rate on the ad: it was $1.99 per minute. And the first three minutes were free. If he kept it down to ten minutes, it could be a deal. He had just been paid. And come on now, he owed it to himself.

He hesitated a bit, and then his hand reached out to the phone. An automated husky voice greeted him and asked him to punch in his credit card number. Rahul thought again – should he go ahead?

After this there was no going back. But then was it not that he who hesitated lost, and a faint heart never won a fair lady? With his heart in his mouth, Rahul punched in his Mastercard. A reassuring voice told him that his card was being authorized and that he would not be charged till three minutes into a conversation with a real girl. Rahul liked the sound of that – nothing sleazy, clean and fair business. In India sleaze means getting ripped off but here in the US there is honour in smut. One of the many things he liked about the country.

A real female voice came on: 'Hi sir, how would you like to be addressed?'

Panicking, Rahul asked: 'Am I being charged from now?'

The friendly voice replied: 'No sir, not yet. I am the pleasure facilitator. (What a beautiful job, Rahul thought.) My job is to know a little bit about what you would like so that we can give you a fantastic experience. Yes sir, so how would you like to be addressed?'

Rahul thought of providing a false identity but then he realized he wanted to be addressed by his own name. It was more personal, and heck, who would ever know? But then again from his experiences in the bars he thought better of it and replied in his best American accent (which he felt was pretty good):

'Bob S...'

'Just first name, please sir. Here we only go by our first names. So Bob, what kind of girl would you like: Swedish exchange-student, Japanese schoolgirl, Russian dominatrix, Vietnamese submissive, all-American cheerleader, or an ebony pleasure-queen?'

Wow, Rahul thought – a buffet of succulent ladies. Sure beats Spice of India's overpriced assortment of stale tandoori chicken and paneer makhni (a treat Rahul allowed himself every alternate weekend) in terms of choice and nourishment.

Three cheers for capitalism.

He thought for a while. Swedish exchange-student reminded him of Bofors. Japanese schoolgirl made him feel uncomfortable. Russian dominatrix made him think of Khruschev. Vietnamese submissive. Naaah...

'How about an all-American cheerleader?'

'Sure, Bob. We aim to please here at 1-900-HOTTIES. Please wait while we redirect the call to your dream date. Your three minutes begin after she picks up the phone. Congratulations again on your most excellent choice. Enjoy.'

Rahul waited with bated breath. This sure beats the hell out of hanging endlessly in places where no one even looked back at you. No time waste, no humiliation – instead instant, hassle-free gratification. He could not believe his luck. In a few seconds he would be speaking to an all-American cheerleader!

Click.

An undecipherable voice. A very thick Southern Texas

accent. Rahul could only make out a 'howdy partner' and the
rest of her words were lost in a mumble.

Rahul kept on repeating in his American accent, 'Could you
please speak a little louder?'

No luck.

He still could not make head or tail of what the girl was
drawling. And in the corner of his brain the clock was ticking.
The free minutes would be over any time now and he had not
yet understood the first thing she was trying to say.

And then straining to hear, he heard the background sound
over which the cheerleader was speaking. There was something
very familiar about the ambient noise but he could not put his
finger on it.

And then it hit him.

He knew that sound: the unmistakable drone of heavy traffic
and riotous blowing of horns.

There was only one country he knew where horns were
blown like this.

India! The penny dropped. The cheats had transferred his
call to India!

Texan beauty indeed.

Under normal circumstances Rahul was all in favour of
outsourcing. For hundreds of years, starting from the time of
the East India Company, India had been at the receiving end
of global trade with its local industries being decimated by
Western competition. This, of course, the pundits said was
not the concomitant of imperialism but of the nature of 'free
markets' which was nothing but a natural extension of Darwin's
theory of evolution. Faced with modern methods of production
and automation, Indian industry had been unable to adapt and
thus had been forced out by the 'fittest'.

Well, now the tide had turned and it was India which could 'out-price' the West in the service and knowledge sector, without the help of political overlordship. Ironically, the same free-market gurus had now become all 'Swadeshi' (desh=USA) protectionists. Of course they do not directly say that India outperformed them (which would be an admission of defeat) but instead chose to point out that the competition between Western firms and Indian ones were not equal as India had lax environmental regulations, child labour, caste system and communal divide. As to why these should be the reasons why the IT engineer in India produced code and provided technical support at a lower cost than his American counterpart, Rahul had not been able to conclusively figure out.

What, however, he figured out was that the 'Your Indian accents are weird' and 'You guys steal our jobs' were driven more from a sense of powerless frustration at the inevitability of global markets than based on sound logic.

But today was different.

Today he was the American with the accent. Today it was he who was expecting 'made in USA' service like any true George Bush-approved patriot.

And today the bastards had 'outsourced' him to India, the place where they had poorly trained personnel with wrong accents and unpronounceable names.

His voice rose: 'Excuse me. Has this call been transferred to India? I demand to know.'

The female voice at the other end immediately changed from the indecipherable Texas accent to clear English.

'I am sorry, sir, but yes your call has been outsourced to India. Actually, to keep operating costs down, the company has had to globalize these calls. Sir, this is just a fantasy – I hope you understand, Amorous Entertainment Ltd, our parent company, has no legal obligation to provide you with the all-American girl you asked for. I apologize for my accent: I normally do the Japanese and the Vietnamese girl – the girl who does the all-American cheerleader has just quit her job. I am really really sorry for this.'

She continued with an amazingly sexy voice. 'However, truth be told, I am from India, the land of the *Kamasutra* where the girls are as lush as the mighty Ganges and know how to please. I can be quite a handful. So tell me, sir, have you ever heard of the flying monkey position? Want me to tell you about it?'

Rahul's initial indignation had been replaced by sympathy. The poor Indian girl must be some beautiful college kid forced to do this because of financial constraints. Maybe her dad had lost his job in a factory lockout. Maybe her mother was seriously ill and needed money for treatment. After all, which Indian girl would ever do such things of her own free will?

And the teary voice of the girl once she had been caught in her lie had aroused the man in Rahul in a way he had not quite imagined he would be aroused. It was not her fault that the Texas girl quit. If he had been a true-blue American he would abuse the poor Indian and hang up. But not Rahul. Even though he wanted to settle in the US at all costs, he still loved his country. And more importantly, its girls. And something about this girl's helplessness also excited him – he wondered why.

Rahul put on his best chivalrous knight tone. Reverting to his own accent so as to put the girl at ease he said: 'Hi, my name is Rahul, not Bob. I am an Indian student too so you need not tell me about the *Kamasutra* – I live by it.' (Well, a white lie, but as she said, this was all a fantasy!)

The girl laughed. A beautiful cadence. Rahul's heart missed a beat. This girl really had an amazingly sexy voice.

She said: 'Hi Rahul, I am Kamna. Really pleased to meet you. So where in India are you from?'

Rahul glanced at the watch. Goddamn this was costing him plenty. More importantly, they had not even talked a bit of what he had paid for. But he liked this – actually this conversation was much more exciting than a few minutes of mechanized huffing and puffing that he would have otherwise hoped to get.

'Baroda,' he replied.

'Hey, Baroda! That is so cool. I am from Baroda too.' Her voice became warmer. They were friends now.

'You must be one of those geniuses who go to the US after their engineering.'

Rahul smiled self-contentedly. That he was, he had to accept. A genius, that is.

What a coincidence, thought Rahul. You have got to hand it to the Americans. They promised him local girls and by Jove, had he got one.

Rahul then launched into a long rant about how lonely he was. For some reason, as a desi talking to another desi he felt he was morally obligated to provide a justification for dialing a sex chat line.

The girl was more than understanding about Rahul's loneliness.

'So don't you have a girlfriend there? Some hot blonde in the US who can look after your needs?'

Rahul sighed. Of course he did not, else why would he be calling her? But he could not make it sound as if he could not. Better to say he would not.

'Well no, Kamna. I prefer brown skin – fairness turns me off.'

The musical voice cooed, 'So Rahul, do you then have any girlfriend in India?'

Rahul was feeling exceedingly honest. Somewhere subconsciously he was falling in lust with this goddess of love. And he needed to start this relationship off by making a clean breast of things.

'No, Kamna, I do not. Well not in the official sense. But yes there was a girl in my locality I used to love. Or I suppose I should be honest and say I had the hots for.'

Kamna giggled. 'My my. Tell me about her. Don't be shy. I know exactly what guys look at when they get the hots for someone. So let's skip the goodness of heart and soundness of character bit. Right?'

Rahul was breathing noticeably heavier now. Oh God, he thought, this lady knew how to press the right buttons. He then launched into a lurid description of a girl who lived in the same housing society and whom he had spent countless nights 'thinking about'. Abetted by encouraging mmms and 'tell me mores' he was soon lost in explicit details of her anatomical attributes.

Rahul's mind did pause to register as to how delectably perverted this conversation had become, but what amazed him was how accepting and understanding this Indian girl was – all the girls he had known growing up were such behenjis, the ones with the 'I will tell teacher' and 'I always took you for a decent sort' on their lips. It was another matter that he was doing all the hot talking, the girl was merely encouraging him to go on and in the end he would have to foot the bill. Which Rahul realized must be quite high now. But he was no longer thinking with his brain.

'Wow, Rahul. Your dream girl seems to be right out of the walls of a Khajuraho temple. So is she the only one who caught your... shall I say... fancy?'

Rahul was talking in an impassioned whisper by now.

'She had an even hotter elder sister. I have often fantasized about both of them. Together.'

The girl giggled again. 'Who would have thought that Mr Brainac here was so colourful. So what were their names? And do tell me about the fantasies involving both of them? If you don't mind, that is.'

Rahul did not mind.

'Sowmya and Anila. Well there was this one time when...'

The girl's tone changed a bit: 'Sowmya and Anila Mirchandani?'

Wait. Was this one of them? Rahul's heart was now turning cartwheels. Could it really be that one of the two goddesses had actually become a phone sex operator? And that he had been talking dirty to one of those unattainable fairies for so long? Well, unattainable they no longer were.

Rahul excitedly replied, 'Yes yes. But how do you know them, Kamna?'

There was silence at the other end. Had the line been cut off? Had the girl been so ashamed of being found out that she had disconnected? Oh no no, please no, good Lord, thought Rahul.

'Hello, hello, are you there?'

The voice had now undergone a Kafkian metamorphosis.

'Bastard. Horny pervert. I know you. You are that pot-bellied idiot who used to stay in No. 24 and would try to peek into our houses. Rahul. Why did I not recognize that name before?

'Go tell your dirty ideas to your own sister, you bastard. You shameless idiot. Take a look at yourself in the mirror even before you think of Sowmya and Anila. One more dirty thought about the two of them, I shall gouge out your hungry eyes and feed them to the crows. Then I shall twist your little thingie out and leave it among the green chillies to dry. You got that, scumbag? Your parents send you to the US to study and this is how you spend your time there – shameless monkey!'

The click of the telephone disconnecting was followed by another automated voice. 'Thank you for using 1-900-HOTTIES. Your credit card has been charged $178.89 including call time, tax and state surcharges. We look forward to your business again. 1-900-Hotties where the possibilities are boundless and satisfaction always guaranteed.'

$178.89. That was almost what Rahul spent on two month's worth of groceries. But money was the last thing on his mind as he sat on the couch – his head in his hands.

This was because it had hit him. He knew who Kamna was. It was Kokila Aunty – the mother of Sowmya and Anila, happy-go-lucky, roly-poly, with oodles of fat bulging at her waist, the local gossip server who offered pujas three times a day. How on God's earth could she be a sex-phone operator? Well, evidently she was and Rahul had just spent $178.89 unloading his darkest fantasies onto a lady pushing the wrong side of fifty, and if that was not bad enough, his reputation in the housing colony was now toast.

He knew very well that if ladies like Kokila Aunty wanted to take down a reputation she could do that effectively without getting herself scorched. He remembered the case of Lamba Uncle, an old bachelor whom he found nice enough but who was whispered to be a gay paedophile. Now the rumour mill had a new goat on the block: 'Rahul, the American pervert'. How was he ever going to go back and look at the mohalla people in the eye?

Oh well, he would just have to cross that bridge when he came to it. With his hands shaking Rahul reached for his laptop. So much code still needed to be written. At least no one here in US knew of this monstrous embarrassment. If there was any saving grace in the whole thing it was this.

'Duuuuuuude.'

Rahul looked up. His apartment mates were standing in the corridor. Rohan was doubled up on the ground laughing and Vikas was staring at Rahul, his mouth open in amazement.

And then Rahul remembered. Rohan and Vikas had said they were going to Walmart that evening to buy an extension handset.

The world had gone very dark.

Epilogue

There is one problem that afflicts us Indians.

We find it difficult to end right.

In bed, we do it too quick.

While making a speech, we do it too late.

And when in power, we never do it at all.

Immensely conscious of this disease that is my birthright and noting how large this book has become, I realize that it is time to wrap up, something I would like to do by thanking all of you who have made it this far, travelling with me on this intensely personal journey through Indian pop culture.

The India we live in is very different from what it was twenty years ago. One wouldn't think so, of course, if one just went by representations of India in the media. That is because a lot of these still conform to the clichéd templates of old – exotic elephant-riding sadhu with a snake around his neck, slum dog popping out of a mound of excreta and running on the streets, with perhaps the cellphone-wielding software engineer consuming empty calories being the latest addition to the box of formulaic prisms through which our country is looked at.

Given that, the objective of the book was to provide a different, radically alternative, *'hatke'* perspective – a perspective through the lens of popular culture.

And with the proliferation of TV channels and the ever-increasing influence of new media, popular culture has become an immensely powerful force shaping and driving the nation, more influential than ever before.

Why so? Simply because in the days of Doordarshan and a few national dailies it required a lot to be famous – like going to the moon or claiming to create oil from water. Popular consciousness took time to evolve. Years after the disco revolution died out in the West, we were still at it, still claiming that we were 'Jimmy Jimmy hep'. Indian music directors could pass off the latest Grammy hits as original creations and be found out ten years later!

Not any more. Now with 24/7 channels, Internet bulletin boards and blogs, we are more plugged into the world than ever before. What is cool and what is not changes from one day to another. Aunties now want to wear low-rise jeans as soon as Britney Spears cavorts in one. And all that is needed to become a national celebrity is a forcible kiss at a birthday party or falling into a well.

This easy attainability of fame has set in motion an epic battle.

A Kurukshetra for the spotlight.

The participants in this fight are as diverse as they can be – groups of people eager to take offence at any and everything, hormonal men vying for the affection of women on social networking sites, politicians with feel-good slogans and carefully crafted media-friendly images, cable news with its 'India at war' sensationalism even when we are playing Bangladesh in cricket, subaltern bards singing about the presence of atom bombs in bustiers, garishly decorated and acted sitcoms, unreal reality shows, pay-per-minute 'party' lines.

What unites them is the desire for the ultimate prize. Namely the power to shape the way you talk, the way you spend, the way you vote, and the way you live.

And so the battle goes on 24/7 as everyone everywhere claws for your mindspace, clambering over each other, with just one thing to say:

'May I Hebb Your Attention Pliss.'

Acknowledgements

'Zindagi mein kuch banna ho, Kuch hasil karna ho, Kuch jeetna ho, To hamesha apne dil ki suno, Aur agar dil se bhi koi jawaab na aaye ... To apni aankhein band karke apni Maa aur Baba ka naam lo ... Phir dekhna tum har manzil paa sakoge, Har mushkil aasan ho jayegi, Jeet tumhari hogi ..... Sirf tumhari...'[1]

—*Kabhi Khushi Kabhi Gam* (from memory)

Mother: 'What! My son wrote a book and he did not even consider thanking his parents. What has the world come to?'

I would first off like to express a debt of gratitude to my parents for their contribution in making me the demented, totally random individual that wrote this book. In the same breath I would also like to thank my grandmother and all those

---

1 English synopsis: If you want to achieve anything in life, listen to your heart. If your heart has stopped beating for some reason, think of your parents. Then you will see you have attained everything you ever wanted.

relatives and friends who collectively are to blame/congratulate for bringing me to this point in the state-space continuum.

Wife: 'What! My husband wrote a book and he did not even consider thanking me. What has the world come to?'

How could I not acknowledge my one-and-only Bhagyawaan who, often unwillingly and under great protest, has shouldered far more responsibility for keeping me fed, clean and healthy over the past few years than she should have – all so that I could watch C-grade Bollywood movies and then review them on my blog?

Indeed. How could I not acknowledge my wife? After all I have to live with her for the rest of my life.

I would also like to doff my imaginary cap to my PhD advisor Dr Rance Cleaveland whose generous research assistantship financed much of the 'research' into the book, research that consisted of hours of Net-surfing, movie-watching, arguing late into the night with other similarly funded PhD students and puking into the toilet. May I never have a research assistant like me.

Thanks to Saugata Mukherjee for his inputs on the book, to Pinaki De for designing the cover and Karthika together with the entire team at HarperCollins, India, for their support.

And finally, an 'Aiiieee Saalaaaaa' shout-out to every reader, commenter, troll and spambot on my blog 'Random Thoughts of a Demented Mind' (http://greatbong.net).

This would not have been possible without you.

If there is even one truly honest sentence in this acknowledgement section, this was it.

I would specifically like to mention those who reviewed chapters for the book and provided vital insights – Aditi Sen, Aseem Chandaver, Atri Bhattacharya, Puloma Mukherjee-

Ghose, Priyanka Nandi, Rituparna Bhowmick, Rohit Pradhan, Ron Dey, Samit Basu, Saurav Mohapatra, Shantanu Bhattacharya, Sharmistha Guha, Shubhadeep Roy, Soumik Sen, Sreyashi Dastidar, Suhel Banerjee and Swati Chaudhuri.

Friend: 'What! Arnab wrote a book and he did not even consider thanking me. What has the world come to?'

I am sorry I missed your name. It was not intentional.

If there is even one truly honest sentence in this acknowledgement section, this was it.